What people are saying about …

THE LIES COUPLES BELIEVE

"Finally! We've been waiting for this book for a long time. Chris Thurman has an ingenious way of helping all of us see the truth behind the lies we too often buy into. Read this insightful book and transform your marriage."

Drs. Les and Leslie Parrott, authors of
Saving Your Marriage Before It Starts

"*The Lies Couples Believe* is one of the most important books a couple could ever read."

Dr. Tim Clinton, president of the American
Association of Christian Counselors

"I have been reading Chris Thurman's wise writings for more than two decades, and I believe *The Lies Couples Believe* is his best yet. In this book, Dr. Thurman explains ways to have a more honest, open, and truly intimate relationship. I highly recommend this book."

Dr. Paul Meier, author and
founder of Meier Clinics

"Marriage, as designed by God, is the closest human relationship possible. This reality increases our vulnerability and unfortunately brings out the darker sides of us as well. Biblically and practically,

Chris clarifies what is going on at a deeper level in a way that will help increase growth and intimacy permanently."

Dr. John Townsend, leadership expert, psychologist, and bestselling author of *Boundaries*

"*The Lies Couples Believe* gives couples a potent and necessary dose of reality and biblical truth. Doing the exercises together can be life changing. I especially appreciated Dr. Thurman's chapter on the lie 'We can reconcile without repenting.' Serious and repetitive sin breaks relationships apart and without forgiveness and genuine repentance, the marriage can never be healed."

Leslie Vernick, counselor, relationship coach, speaker, and bestselling author of *The Emotionally Destructive Marriage*

"I am thrilled to finally hold in my hands a copy of *The Lies Couples Believe*. Chris presents the marital lies with the wisdom of an experienced counselor and the humility of a fellow struggler. Regardless of whether you are engaged, newly married, or married in the double digits, this book should be required reading for every couple who wants to have a happy and healthy marriage."

Vicki Courtney, speaker and bestselling author of *Ever After* and *Move On*

THE *LIES*
COUPLES
BELIEVE

*HOW LIVING THE TRUTH
TRANSFORMS YOUR MARRIAGE*

DR. CHRIS
THURMAN

transforming lives together

THE LIES COUPLES BELIEVE
Published by David C Cook
4050 Lee Vance View
Colorado Springs, CO 80918 U.S.A.

David C Cook Distribution Canada
55 Woodslee Avenue, Paris, Ontario, Canada N3L 3E5

David C Cook U.K., Kingsway Communications
Eastbourne, East Sussex BN23 6NT, England

The graphic circle C logo is a registered trademark of David C Cook.

The website addresses recommended throughout this book are offered as a
resource to you. These websites are not intended in any way to be or imply an
endorsement on the part of David C Cook, nor do we vouch for their content.

Unless otherwise noted, all Scripture quotations are taken from the Holy Bible, New
International Version®, NIV®. Copyright © 1973, 2011 by Biblica, Inc.® Used
by permission of Zondervan. All rights reserved worldwide. www.zondervan.com.
Scripture quotations marked CEV are taken from the Contemporary English
Version © 1991, 1995 by American Bible Society. Used by permission; NASB
are taken from the New American Standard Bible®, Copyright © 1960, 1995
by The Lockman Foundation. Used by permission. (www.Lockman.org);
NKJV are taken from the New King James Version®. Copyright © 1982 by
Thomas Nelson, Inc. Used by permission. All rights reserved; NRSV are taken
from the New Revised Standard Version Bible, copyright 1989, Division of
Christian Education of the National Council of the Churches of Christ in
the United States of America. Used by permission. All rights reserved.
The author has added italics to Scripture quotations for emphasis.

LCCN 2015933706
ISBN 978-1-4347-0905-9
eISBN 978-0-7814-1367-1

© 2015 Christopher Wyatt Thurman
Published in association with the literary agency of D.C. Jacobson &
Associates LLC, an Author Management Company. www.dcjacobson.com.

The Team: Ingrid Beck, Liz Heaney, Amy Konyndyk,
Helen Macdonald, Karen Athen
Cover Design: Nick Lee

Printed in the United States of America
First Edition 2015

2 3 4 5 6 7 8 9 10

072915cs

To Holly
I am a very rich man because of you.

A wife of noble character who can find?
She is worth far more than rubies.

—Proverbs 31:10

CONTENTS

ACKNOWLEDGMENTS

Getting to write this book feels like being given a great honor, then having only a minute or so to thank everyone before the orchestra starts playing and I'm ushered off the stage. So, I'll do my best. Please forgive me if I forget anyone.

I want to start by thanking all the couples I have counseled over the years. Thank you for trusting me with your relationship, thank you for taking my counsel to heart, thank you for courageously facing your weaknesses as a spouse, thank you for teaching me so much more about holy matrimony than I taught you, and thank you for graciously allowing me to make mistakes in how I counseled you at times. Thank you for blessing me with the privilege of helping you have a loving and vibrant marriage, the kind of marriage God wants you to have.

I want to thank my literary agent, Don Jacobson, for believing that God has given me an important message for couples who want to make their marriages all they were meant to be. Don, thanks for all you and your team have done to help me express what God has put on my heart. Thanks to Vicki Courtney for believing I had something of value to say to people who are struggling in life and for encouraging me to write again. Vicki, you are a true godsend, and I appreciate your encouragement more than you know.

I greatly appreciate the wonderful people at David C Cook who took a chance on an author who hadn't written a book in almost two decades. I am truly grateful for your belief in me and your confidence that this book will find a place in the crowded world of Christian books on marriage. Thanks to my editor, Liz Heaney, for the great job she did making what I wrote so much better. Liz, everything you suggested was spot-on and pushed me to a much-higher level as a writer.

I am thankful for my professional colleague and friend Dr. Steve Stratton. Steve, thank you for showing me what it looks like to be a Christian psychologist who practices his craft with excellence—and for inspiring me to do the same.

I am so very grateful for my wife, Holly. We have been married for thirty-four years, and as you will learn from reading this book, I am not an easy person to be married to. Holly, more than anyone else on this planet, you have helped me understand what grace looks like and thus have helped me better understand what God is like. I will never be able to thank you enough for your love and support over our many years together. If we lay up treasures in heaven by faithfully loving others down here on earth, you have incredible riches waiting on you.

To my son, Matt, and his wife, Nicole; my daughter Ashley and her husband, David; and my daughter Kelly—thank you for being the most incredible kids and kids-in-law a dad could have. I am so proud of each of you and the many ways you have made the world a better place to live. Ashley and David, thanks for giving your mom and me Scout, the most incredible granddaughter on the planet. Miss Scout, when you read this book years from now, perhaps as you are considering walking down the aisle with some guy who is nowhere near good enough for you (because no one will be), I want you to know how thankful I am that you are here and how much incredible joy you have brought into my life.

At awards shows and sporting events, people often express their heartfelt appreciation to God for the honor that was bestowed on them or the victory that was won. I want to add my voice to that list of people. I am sixty-one as I write these words, and looking back on my life, I see God's blessings at every turn: getting into graduate school to fulfill a dream of becoming a psychologist when I was a less-than-spectacular student, marrying a wonderful woman when I was anything but a wonderful man, having the privilege of parenting three incredible children when I didn't know what in the world I was doing, and having the opportunity to write books when I am not a writer by gift or talent. Everywhere I look in my life, I see God being not only the one who gave me these wonderful opportunities, but also the one who helped all of them turn out so well. God, words can never adequately express how truly grateful I am, but thank You. Thank You so much for loving this particular ragamuffin and showering him with so many extravagant blessings.

Chris Thurman, Austin, Texas
January 2015

INTRODUCTION

When I got married thirty-four years ago, I wasn't a very good husband. Let me explain.

During my childhood years, my dad was in the military, so our home had "a place for everything and everything in its place." And everything that was in its proper place was polished, folded, cleaned, shined, vacuumed, swept, waxed, washed, or Windexed. Put all of this together with my natural bent toward perfectionism and I had the perfect storm for becoming a person who cared way too much about order, cleanliness, and upkeep. Consequently, when Holly and I married, I expected her to put everything where it belonged, keep things so clean you could eat off the floor, and take really good care of what little we owned. If you are getting the impression that living with me was "no day at the park," you would be correct.

So in the early years of our marriage, I reacted in a not-so-wonderful way when I would come home and find Holly's shoes in the middle of the living-room floor, her coat hanging on a doorknob, her purse in the kitchen sink (I'm not making that up), and Holly looking everywhere for the car keys she had lost for the zillionth time. Holly had violated Military Marital Law 329.64: "Thou shalt not leaveth thy things where they do not belongeth, faileth to taketh good careth of them, and not knowest where they are-ith" (obviously that's the King James Version). In my mind, Holly had engaged in "conduct unbecoming a wife" and needed to change posthaste if she wanted to avoid having an unhappy husband on her hands for the rest of her life.

What is painfully clear to me now is that I was the one who had the more serious problem. I wrongly believed that *my spouse should be just like me* and that *my spouse is a bigger mess of a human being than I am*—two marital lies we will explore in the chapters to come. These faulty beliefs kept me from seeing that Holly was actually supposed to be the person *God* wanted her to be (I sometimes get God and me confused), and that I didn't have my act together any more than she did. When we married, all she did was leave her stuff lying around the house. I, on the other hand, stomped around throwing a childish hissy fit when Holly wasn't exactly the way I thought she should be. I wish I could go back in time and change my faulty ways of thinking and treat Holly the way a husband in his right mind is supposed to treat his wife.

Marriage is made or broken by many things, but the lies we believe about this most sacred of all relationships significantly contribute to marital disconnection and disharmony. When you have faulty beliefs about marriage, you will treat your spouse in hurtful and wounding ways. However, when you believe "whatever is true, whatever is noble, whatever is right, whatever is pure, whatever is lovely, whatever is admirable" (Phil. 4:8) about marriage, you will treat your spouse in loving and kind ways.

Given this book's title, I assume you are reading this because you are curious about whether you and your spouse have faulty beliefs about marriage. I can assure you that you do. All of us do. Sadly, the majority of us don't see all the wrongheaded views we have about holy matrimony and how they cause us to mistreat our spouses. I certainly didn't recognize the lies I believed about marriage when I walked down the aisle, and I surely didn't make the connection between my "crazy" ways of thinking and how I wounded my wife at times. I hope what I have written in this book will help you gain greater awareness of the faulty beliefs you, too, have about marriage. But most of all, I hope you will experience renewed dedication to living out the truth in your marriage so that you can be a more loving spouse.

I would like to share a few caveats:

One, this is not a book about positive thinking in marriage. I don't believe in positive thinking (or, for that matter, negative thinking). I see positive thinking as pop psychology, New Age nonsense. In the chapters to come, you'll see that I am not the least bit concerned about whether a belief happens to be positive or negative. In this book I share my deep concern about one thing and one thing only: Are the beliefs you have about marriage true?

Two, while I steer you away from focusing on how your spouse treats you, I am not suggesting you put up with abuse. If your spouse treats you cruelly or violently, do not tolerate it. Establish clear and nonnegotiable boundaries. Draw a firm line in the sand regarding abusive behavior, and respond strongly and courageously when that line is crossed.

Three, knowledge of the truth doesn't necessarily lead to lasting change in people. It's a nice start, but it won't get the job done in transforming your marriage. The Bible warns, "Do not merely listen to the word, and so deceive yourselves. Do what it says" (James 1:22). For your marriage to improve, you have to act on the truth, not just intellectually agree with it. And although I wrote this book with the primary focus of helping you improve your *attitude* so that you will *act* toward your spouse in a more loving and caring manner, I also hoped it would significantly influence your *affections* toward your spouse (in the direction of greater feelings of tenderness, compassion, fondness, and warmth).

Finally, I'm convinced that every one of us who is married believes all ten of the lies covered in this book. We believe some of these lies more strongly than others, but we believe all of them to some degree. If after reading this book you find you and your spouse continue to experience a great deal of conflict and distress in your marriage, then I urge you to go to marital counseling with a trained therapist who can help you understand the issues and how to overcome them.

I am confident your desire to "be transformed by the renewing of your mind" (Rom. 12:2) in marriage will be empowered by God, who is always "at work in you, both to will and to work for His good pleasure" (Phil. 2:13 NASB). Take my word for it: if God could straighten out the beliefs of this attitudinally challenged husband, He can certainly do the same for you.

Now, with no further ado, let's go on this journey together and see what God is ready, willing, and able to do to help us have marriages that are richer and deeper than we could have ever hoped for or imagined.

CHAPTER 1

ATTITUDE IS EVERYTHING IN MARRIAGE

The longer I live, the more I realize the impact of attitude on life. Attitude, to me, is more important than facts. It is more important than the past, than education, than money, than circumstances, than failure, than success, than what other people think or say or do. It is more important than appearance, giftedness or skill. It will make or break a company ... a church ... a home. The remarkable thing is we have a choice every day regarding the attitude we will embrace for that day.

—Charles R. Swindoll

In your relationships with one another, have the same mindset as Christ Jesus.

—Philippians 2:5

"I feel like I do everything around here, and when I ask you for help, you don't pay attention!" Julie said, her voice rising in frustration.

"I'm not sure what you're talking about," Mike said, feeling defensive.

"Well, the other night I asked you to help me put the kids to bed, and you just kept working on your laptop while watching television."

"I thought you knew I was fighting a deadline at work and that I couldn't stop what I was doing."

"Well, you didn't make that very clear … All you did was grunt at me … and you still could have stopped for a few minutes to help me out."

"Julie, you knew I was under the gun at work and that I didn't have the time to help you out with the kids."

"You can't help me out even when you have a lot of work to do? I'm just as stressed out and busy as you are!"

"If I don't stay on top of things at work, I don't have a job and we don't have an income! So can you cut me a little slack?"

"Mike, I don't mind cutting you some slack. I just think you use work as an excuse to not help me out with the kids."

"Maybe I do, but that wasn't the case the other night."

"Okay, but I would appreciate it if you would at least let me know more clearly when you aren't going to help. Grunting at me isn't going to work."

Sound familiar? If you're married, you've probably had a conversation like this with your spouse more than a few times. If you were to ask Mike and Julie what caused their conflict, you would probably get two different answers. Julie would tell you Mike doesn't help her around the house enough and uses pressure at work to justify it. Mike would tell you Julie expects way too much and is not very understanding about the stress he is under. Unfortunately, both would agree on one thing: the problem in their marriage is *the other person*, and if he or she would just be more loving and caring, all their marital troubles would disappear.

To a certain degree, Mike and Julie are right. A major problem in their marriage (and every marriage) is that neither spouse treats the other in a fully loving manner, and Mike and Julie's marriage isn't going to improve much until they begin to treat each other with more care and consideration. But I say "to a certain degree" because neither Mike nor Julie see the other major problem in their marriage.

This book is about the other major problem—faulty beliefs, attitudes, and expectations. Simply put, it is about the lies we believe in regard to marriage. All of us enter marriage believing certain lies about holy matrimony, and these lies can cause our marriages to become unholy messes. This is what is happening to Mike and Julie. They have a disappointing and disconnected relationship because they have flawed ways of thinking about marriage, which leads them to treat each other poorly at times. As long as these faulty beliefs stay hidden and remain unchanged, Mike and Julie will continue to be stuck in a frustrating and intimacy-damaging dance with each other.

The bottom line of this book is this: Your attitudes and expectations are important in determining the kind of relationship you have as husband and wife. The right attitude can help you create a loving marriage, and the wrong attitude can help you create an unloving one. And here's the deal: You each get to decide what your beliefs and expectations in marriage are going to be. God has left that choice totally up to you.

MARRIAGE: YOUR WAY OR GOD'S WAY?

If you reread the Bible with fresh eyes, you may get the impression that God seems more concerned about changing people's attitudes than about rescuing them from difficult situations. I'm not saying God's heart doesn't break when He sees us in dire straits. I know He cares deeply about us. Nor am I saying God doesn't want us to ask for help. I know God wants us to turn to Him when we are going through rough times (and when things are good). I'm simply suggesting that God wants to help us develop the right perspective about painful circumstances just as much as He wants to remove us from them.

Think for a minute about some of the most well-known events recorded in the Bible: Jonah was thrown overboard and spent three days inside the belly of a large fish because he refused to prophesy against the city of Nineveh (think Las Vegas on steroids); Job, a righteous and God-fearing man, was undeservedly stripped of his family, health, and possessions; Joseph, the apple of his father's eye, was sold into slavery by his envious, hate-filled brothers; Esther, as a young woman, was forced to become a member of King Xerxes's harem, and, a year later, the king's wife; and Abraham was asked to sacrifice his long-awaited and much-beloved son, Isaac. While all of these people were dealing with traumatic events and were in crisis, they all had one thing in common: they wanted relief from the situations they were in, but God allowed them to go through them so that He could bring about a deep and lasting change in their attitudes.

Most of us want God to protect us from the difficulties and challenges of life. We don't want Him to allow us to go through hard times so that He can work on straightening out our perspective. The dynamic here is analogous to the relationship between parent and child. When children complain about having to eat broccoli for dinner, they don't want to hear their mom or dad say, "You need to have a better attitude about broccoli." Children just don't want to eat their broccoli, and they are not receptive to being told their attitude needs to improve or that dessert is going to be withheld until it does.

Similarly, when our spouses disappoint or hurt us, we often complain to God and demand either that He miraculously change them or, if things don't get better, that He give us permission to find someone else. What we don't want to hear God say is, "You need to have a better attitude about your spouse." Yes, that's pretty much the last thing we want to hear.

I believe marriage is one of the most difficult challenges we go through in life. I'm sure you've heard the joke, "There are three rings in marriage: the engagement ring, the wedding ring, and the *suffering*." Well, that joke carries, pun intended, a ring of truth to it. But I don't think the main issue to God is that marriage is hard. The main issue to God seems to be that we approach our marital disappointments and conflicts as iron-sharpening-iron opportunities (Prov. 27:17) that He can use to overhaul our faulty beliefs and help us learn to love our spouses "as Christ loved the church and gave himself up for her" (Eph. 5:25).

When it comes to marriage, it is crucial we understand that God is more focused on changing our faulty beliefs, attitudes, and expectations than He is on removing us from the difficult situations we go through. After all, God doesn't say, "Take captive every *event*"; He says, "Take captive every *thought*" (2 Cor. 10:5). God doesn't say, "Whatever *situations* are true, noble, right, pure, lovely, and admirable, think about *such situations*"; He says, "Whatever *is* true, noble, right, pure, lovely, and admirable, think about *such things*" (see Phil. 4:8). God doesn't say, "Be transformed by the renewing of your *circumstances*"; He says, "Be transformed by the renewing of your *mind*" (Rom. 12:2). Developing the right beliefs is as important as anything else God is doing to help you and your spouse have a healthy marriage.

Now I don't want you to misinterpret what I'm saying here. I'm not saying that changing your beliefs and attitudes about marriage is the *only* way or even the *best* way to strengthen your marriage. God gives us all kinds of ways to develop a loving and joyful marriage: "Confess your sins to each other" (James 5:16), "[forgive] each other" (Eph. 4:32), "submit to one another" (Eph. 5:21), "[speak] the truth in love" (Eph. 4:15), make every effort to be at peace (Rom. 12:18), be gentle and patient (Eph. 4:2), "be kind and compassionate" (Eph. 4:32), put away all bitterness and anger (Eph. 4:31), humble ourselves (1 Pet. 5:6), "serve one another" (Gal. 5:13), "be quick to listen, slow to speak and slow to become angry" (James 1:19), and have genuine sorrow about the hurtful things we do and stop doing them (2 Cor. 7:10). If you are going to have a marriage that pleases God, applying these and other principles in the Bible is just as important as developing the right beliefs.

However, couples often make the mistake of overlooking, if not ignoring altogether, the importance of changing their faulty beliefs as a way to become more loving toward their spouses. In his book *Abounding Grace*, psychiatrist M. Scott Peck put it much better than I could:

> I suspect that most people, if asked, would proclaim love to be the greatest of the virtues. But I am not so sure. There is no question that love will make many more thoughtful—that love is the force propelling them to stretch their minds on behalf of their beloved. Yet I know of many instances where by thinking deeply, women and men have been led to become more empathetic, more compassionate, more loving. It is unclear to me whether there is not enough love in the world or whether there is not enough good thinking. As I think about it, however, it is not an either/or matter. Rather we might suppose that these two— real love and real thinking—go hand in hand, operating in tandem.[1]

True love and right thinking go hand in hand. They always have, and they always will. You cannot separate the two, and attempting to do so will damage your marriage. To love right, you have to think right. To think right, you have to love right. This book is going to help you with both so that your marriage can be everything God meant it to be.

THE THREE ENEMIES OF RIGHT THINKING

Before we go any further, I want to warn you about three enemies who will try to thwart your efforts to replace wrong beliefs with the right beliefs in marriage. Each enemy is formidable and won't go down without a fight.

The first enemy is you. Ever since Adam and Eve sampled forbidden fruit, human beings have had a fallen bent toward misperceiving reality and believing things that are untrue. Blame Adam and Eve if you want, but on the day they disobeyed God, our ability to think "right" (accurately, correctly, rationally, truthfully) went straight into the ditch, and we are going to remain in that ditch until God takes us home to heaven where we receive a brand-new body with a flawless "thinker" in it. Like it or not, the expression "I'm my own worst enemy" has a great deal of truth to it, especially when it comes to our tendency to misperceive reality. Here, we have met the enemy, and it is us.

The second enemy is the world. The seven billion people who populate the planet have a vast array of faulty philosophies and perspectives that they have contributed to the marketplace of ideas, as if each were etched-in-stone truth. The apostle Paul prophetically noted, "For the time will come when people will not put up with sound doctrine. Instead, to suit their own desires, they will gather around them a great number of teachers to say what their itching ears want to hear. They will turn their ears away from the truth and turn aside to myths" (2 Tim. 4:3–4). Here, we have met the enemy, and it is "they say."

The third enemy is Satan. This may sound like a bunch of spiritual mumbo jumbo, but that is exactly what Satan and his minions want it to sound like. Satan wants us to believe he doesn't exist, or if we know he does, he doesn't want us to take him seriously. I'm not one to suggest that Satan is under every rock, but I believe he is under most of them. Here, we have met the Enemy, and he is called "the father of lies" (John 8:44) and "the deceiver" (Rev. 12:9 NRSV). A primary part of his job description is to whisper deadly falsehoods in your ear every day in an effort "to steal and kill and destroy" (John 10:10) you and your relationships with those you love.

If you want a healthy and vibrant marriage, you have to change the faulty beliefs and attitudes you have about this sacred relationship. This book is my effort to help you identify the most damaging lies couples believe about marriage, lies that come from a lethal combination of your own faulty beliefs, the world's distorted views, and Satan's falsehoods. I want to help you become aware of your faulty thinking so that you can exchange lies with truth and strengthen your marriage. And I want to help you as a couple live out the truth in front of your children so that they don't end up as confused about marriage as you may have been when you walked down the aisle.

ASSESSING YOUR LIES, PUTTING TRUTH INTO ACTION

Take a few minutes to respond to the questionnaire below, using the scale provided. Please make sure you don't answer from your "head" regarding what you think the right answer is—answer from your "gut" about what you honestly believe.

Strongly Disagree 1 2 3 4 5 6 7 Strongly Agree

_____ 1. The purpose of marriage is to be happy.

_____ 2. My spouse can completely meet all my needs.

_____ 3. My spouse is a bigger mess of a human being than I am.

_____ 4. I am entitled to my spouse's love.

_____ 5. Our marital problems are all my spouse's fault.

_____ 6. My spouse should accept me just the way I am.

_____ 7. My spouse should be just like me.

_____ 8. I see my spouse for who my spouse really is.

_____ 9. My spouse has to earn my forgiveness.

_____ 10. We can reconcile without repenting.

Now look back through your answers and circle your three highest scores. Most likely, these are the lies that hold you in the greatest degree of bondage in terms of how you view your marriage, and they are probably the ones causing the most damage to you and your spouse. To have a loving and intimate marriage, you have to replace the lies you believe with truth. A marriage that truly pleases God is one in which you allow Him to change your attitude so that it becomes "the same mindset as Christ Jesus" (Phil. 2:5), enabling you to love your spouse in the same life-changing way God loves you.

In order to help you not only "listen to the word" but also "do what it says" (James 1:22), I've included some exercises at the end of every chapter. If you complete them, they can help improve your marriage. As you work through the exercises, *don't rely on your own abilities and strengths. Instead, please ask God to empower you to change.* Our fallen minds, wills, and emotions are simply not up to the task of getting the job done. Every one of us needs supernatural help when we try to change, and we need it badly. Remember: "Unless the LORD builds the house, the builders labor in vain" (Ps. 127:1).

The exercises will involve practicing the five As of intimacy repair, which I've named the "Fair" method. The five As are as follows:

1. Acknowledge
2. Assess
3. Adopt
4. Act
5. Ask

First, **Acknowledge** you believe the lie the chapter focuses on, even if you believe it only to a small degree. You can't change something if you refuse to admit you have a problem with it. As the joke goes, "Denial is not a river in Egypt." So consider the degree to which you have bought into each lie. Forgive my candor, but if you think certain lies in this book don't apply to you, you're lying to yourself.

Second, **Assess** the damage caused by believing this lie. List all the spiritual, emotional, sexual, physical, and even financial damage this lie has caused in your marriage. For example, if you believe the lie that marriage should make you happy (chapter 2), you will find yourself feeling bitter and resentful toward your spouse when he or she does something you are unhappy about. Your unhappiness may lead you to treat your spouse badly—by withdrawing, being critical, withholding how your spouse wants to be loved—or it may lead you to addictively self-medicating the emotional pain you are in. Every lie comes with a destructive price tag.

Third, **Adopt** verses or passages out of the Bible that speak clearly and directly to the lie. By this I mean look for verses that oppose the lie, and then *memorize and meditate* on those verses so that God, as He tries to free you from believing a particular falsehood, has truth to work with in your mind. If you have a hard time searching out scriptures to counter a given lie, don't worry. In each chapter, I will give you suggestions for verses that will help you defeat the lies.

Fourth, **Act** on the truth you have adopted. I will also help you with this throughout the book, but I want you to take responsibility for making changes in how you treat your spouse. For example, if you have wrongly expected your spouse to meet all your needs, I want you to work on meeting your spouse's needs instead. Your behavior toward your spouse needs to have noticeably changed in a positive direction by the time you finish reading this book. If it hasn't, you have not fully yielded to the Holy Spirit's efforts to "guide you into all the truth" (John 16:13) and "convict the world concerning sin" (John 16:8 NASB).

Finally, **Ask** for your spouse's forgiveness. The Bible clearly says that we are to "confess [our] sins to one another" (James 5:16 NASB) and "[forgive] each other" (Eph. 4:32). Doing so will keep you humble and on the path to becoming a more loving spouse. Far too many of us never ask our spouses to forgive us for how we mistreat them, and the unwillingness to do so is a death knell to our marriages being able to heal. A word of caution: If you are not truly sorry you have believed these lies or for the damage they have led to, don't ask your spouse to forgive you. Go back to God and earnestly ask Him to help you get there.

If all of this sounds a bit daunting, remember God is on your side and God is *omni*. God is omniscient (all-knowing), which means that He knows absolutely everything there is to know and that everything He knows is "the truth, the whole truth, and nothing but the truth." So, you don't have to wonder if the things God tells you are true—they are. God is also omnipotent (all-powerful), which means that He can do anything He wants to do and has everything under control. So, you don't have to wonder if God has the power to help you change or the desire to do so—He does. Finally, God is omnipresent (everywhere at once), which means the fullness of God is in every nook and cranny of the universe. So, you don't have to wonder if God is with you at all times—He is. If God were not all-knowing, all-powerful, and everywhere at once, we would all be up the marital creek without a paddle and there would be no true hope for our marriages to heal.

Before you go on to the next chapter, I want to compliment you. You don't have to read a book about faulty beliefs and attitudes in marriage, but you are. You don't have to let yourself be challenged about your marital expectations, but you are. You don't have to let God use this book to help you develop a better attitude about marriage, but you are. So, here's a hearty "atta girl" and "atta boy" for the courage you have shown. As we say here in Texas, "Ya dun good!"

Let's examine the lies we believe about marriage and see what God has to say about them. I'll see you in chapter 2.

PRAYER

God, please remove the scales from my eyes that keep me from seeing and believing the truth. Help me admit that many of the beliefs I have about marriage are at odds with how You view this sacred relationship, and help me acknowledge that these faulty views are causing damage to me and my spouse. I want to increasingly walk in the light of Your truth each day. Help me not to stubbornly cling to falsehoods and resist Your efforts to transform my mind, my life, and my marriage. Please help me humbly submit to Your truth so that You can use it to set me free. Thank You, God, that You are Truth and that there is no hint of falsehood, inaccuracy, or distortion in You or in anything You say. I believe the things You say, but help me in my unbelief. In the precious name of Jesus Christ and by the power of the Holy Spirit. Amen.

CHAPTER 2

AND THEY LIVED HAPPILY EVER AFTER

Lie #1: The purpose of marriage is to be happy

*Happiness is like a butterfly; the more you chase
it, the more it will elude you, but if you
turn your attention to other things, it will
come and sit softly on your shoulders.*
—Henry David Thoreau

*In their hearts they say,
"Nothing can hurt us!
We'll always be happy
and free from trouble."*
—Psalm 10:6 (CEV)

The Turtles were a popular group in the mid-to-late 1960s. They had a number of hit songs during their career, but their biggest was "Happy Together." It topped the American charts for three weeks in 1967, knocking the Beatles' "Penny Lane" out of the number one spot.[1] It has been used in numerous movies (*Ernest Goes to Camp*, *Muriel's Wedding*, and *27 Dresses*); television shows (*The Simpsons*, *The Muppet Show*, *ER*, and *The Wonder Years*); and advertisements (Toyota and Ford have used it to sell cars). It has been sung by artists from Donny Osmond to Britney Spears. "Happy Together" has been played about five million times on American radio, and, in 1999, Broadcast Music Inc. (BMI) ranked it as the forty-fourth most performed song in the United States during the twentieth century.[2]

Do you remember the opening lines?

Imagine me and you, I do
I think about you day and night, it's only right
To think about the girl you love, and hold her tight
So happy together[3]

The first time I heard "Happy Together," I was a pimple-faced fourteen-year-old living in east Texas with my mom and brothers while my dad served in Vietnam. I was in the throes of a serious case of puberty and would fall head over heels in love when I had a crush on a girl (which was pretty much all the time). "Happy Together" was one of my favorite songs when I was young and remains so to this day.

Unfortunately, woven into the lyrics of "Happy Together" is a seductive lie that is in a lot of the songs, movies, and romance novels we experience as we transition from childhood through adolescence to young adulthood. For the sake of our marriages, it is critical that we see just how destructive this particular lie is to our marriages and that we disentangle ourselves from it.

THE LIE: BEING IN LOVE AND FEELING HAPPY ARE THE MOST IMPORTANT THINGS IN MARRIAGE

I think being in love and feeling happy are wonderful things. I really do. Nothing else in life can put that bugs-collecting-in-your-teeth smile on your face. But you cannot afford to make being in love and feeling happy *the main focus* of your marriage. If you do, then you have astronomically increased the likelihood that you'll be unhappily married.

Here's why: being in love and feeling happy in marriage are tied to how your spouse treats you. And, like it or not, even the most loving husband or wife will treat you badly on occasion. All of us will, at times, wound our spouses by mistreating them. Count on it. At times your spouse will treat you less like a human being and more like an unruly house pet that just tore up a brand-new sofa. So, if you tie your happiness to how your spouse treats you, you will find yourself feeling unhappy each and every day of the week and twice on Sunday. Your emotional well-being will be all over the map.

Let me give you the worst-case scenario of what I'm talking about. My wife, Holly, loves those television shows in which someone commits a horrible crime and gets caught by dedicated law enforcement professionals. A lot of the episodes are about someone who kills his or her spouse (hmm, now that I think about it, Holly may be watching the show to get some ideas … not that I blame her). The plotline of these episodes follows this predictable pattern:

- I fell madly in love with you and was incredibly happy.
- I assumed that falling in love with you and being incredibly happy meant I was supposed to marry you, so I did.
- Your numerous character flaws and defects, all of which you hid from me before we got married, became evident to me after we married.
- I fell madly out of love with you and became incredibly unhappy.
- I demanded that you make some major changes in who you are.
- You told me what I could do with my demands.
- I became bitter and resentful.
- I decided you weren't going to make it to your next birthday.
- I ended your life, thinking that no one would figure out it was me even though I tripled your life insurance a couple of months before I murdered you and left my DNA all over the crime scene.
- I'm currently serving a life sentence without the possibility of parole and am even more unhappy than when we were married.

Of course, the majority of people who are unhappily married don't murder their spouses (think about it, yes; do it, no). But a fair number of people who are unhappy in their marriages seem to have no problem doing something almost as tragic: murdering their spouses' hearts through constant criticism, condemnation, coldness, and contempt. When you make happiness an idol in marriage, a god before God (Exod. 20:3), you give Satan all the room he needs to "steal and kill and destroy" (John 10:10) your relationship with your spouse.

Don't bypass the high cost of believing this lie. When happiness is the focus of your marriage, not only will you become quite unhappy, but you will also take your unhappiness out on your spouse. Misery loves company; it always has and always will. Because you believe your spouse is the cause of your unhappiness, you will find yourself being critical, demeaning, and even hateful at times so that your mate will be miserable along with you. And you will be tempted to self-medicate your unhappiness, a situation that will put you at greater risk of becoming addicted to self-destructive behavior (overeating, overspending, drinking excessively, taking drugs, spending too much time on the computer, and acting out sexually). The price tag is incredibly high for believing the lie that your happiness is the most important thing in marriage. Don't be foolish enough to ruin your life and your marriage by believing something so grossly untrue.

Please, don't think I am knocking being in love and feeling happy. I believe God has wired our brains in such a way that we are meant to experience and enjoy these wonderful emotions toward our spouses. Also, please don't hear me say you should ever let go of wanting to be in love with your spouse or to feel blissfully happy in his or her arms. What I am saying is this: *the euphoric experience of being in love and the incredible happiness that goes along with it cannot be the central focus of a healthy marriage.*

The world we live in seems to believe that falling in love and being happy are the goals in relationships with the opposite sex, and that once we marry, we should live "happily ever after." If we foolishly believe these lies, we are more willing to end a marriage when we "fall out of love" and are unhappy. In the meantime, our children watch all of this unfold, and they learn that marriage isn't about commitment, loyalty, hard work, and sacrifice, but rather it's about selfish desires—to be in love and be happy—no matter the cost to anyone else.

So, if the main purpose of marriage isn't to be in love and feel happy, what is?

... AND THE TRUTH ABOUT MARRIAGE WILL SET YOU FREE

I believe God has three primary purposes for marriage: companionship, children, and change. I will walk you briefly through the first two and then focus more on the third.

1. Companionship. When God looked at Adam's situation in the garden, He said, "It is not good for the man to be alone" (Gen. 2:18). God was sensitive to the fact that Adam had no other human being to share his life with, that there was "no suitable helper" (Gen. 2:20) for Adam to be close to. So God created Eve in order for Adam to have a lifelong companion he could be intimate with spiritually, emotionally, and sexually.

2. Children. God commanded Adam and Eve to "be fruitful and increase in number" (Gen. 1:28). God made us male and female so that in the context of a committed marital relationship, we could fill the earth with other human beings and "rule over the fish in the sea and the birds in the sky and over every living creature that moves on the ground" (Gen. 1:28). God wanted Adam and Eve to have children, for their children to have children, for their children's children … okay, you get the point.

3. *Change.* God uses marriage to help husbands and wives become more whole and complete. Ever since Adam and Eve sinned, human beings haven't been "right" spiritually, psychologically, sexually, and physically. Marriage is one of the most important ways God tries to take you from being a real mess of a human being to a real work of art. God uses a husband and a wife "as iron sharpens iron" (Prov. 27:17) to help each other become "mature and complete, not lacking anything" (James 1:4).

While our world glorifies the idea that intimate relationships are all about being in love and feeling happy, God calls us toward a different kind of love. The most important kind of love we are to have for our spouses is *agape* love. Agape love focuses on helping our husbands or wives become the fullest expression of who God intended them to be.

M. Scott Peck, in his book *The Road Less Traveled*, said love is "the will to extend one's self for the purpose of nurturing one's own or another's spiritual growth."[4]

Here's how I think Peck's definition of love can shine light on what agape love is:

- It comes out of your will, not your emotions or
  your sexual longings toward a person.

- It has a specific goal in mind; it isn't aimless.
- It isn't coercive, manipulative, or controlling; it doesn't force itself on others.
- It attempts to help your loved one grow and mature in a healthy direction; it tries to help your spouse become the Christlike person God meant him or her to be.

So here's the bottom line: *God joined you and your spouse together in holy matrimony so that, as an act of your will, you would facilitate each other's growth toward becoming more fully loving and whole human beings.* If you have agape love for your spouse, you will not be concerned with whether you or your spouse is "in love" or happy. You will focus on helping your spouse move in the direction of becoming more like Christ, the only perfectly loving and whole person to ever walk the planet. Being in love and feeling happy in marriage, though certainly not unimportant and to be enjoyed whenever possible, will be a secondary matter.

Let me drive this home with an analogy. I took up golf about fifteen years ago. Let's assume for a minute that God was the one who wanted me to play golf (which I, however self-servingly, believe to be true). Now, let's ask the million-dollar question: Why did God want me to play golf? Initially, I thought it was because God wanted me to be happy. But once I started playing, I quickly realized my error. How did I know? I was *really unhappy* when I first started playing golf because I was *really bad* at it.

I've come to realize that golf is not designed to make golfers happy. Golf is designed to make golfers *really unhappy* and, as a result, motivate them to become better golfers who are "mature and complete, not lacking anything" (James 1:4). I believe God wanted me to play golf because He wanted to use that particular sport to help me grow as a person, both spiritually and psychologically (which, by the way, I don't always appreciate!). Now when I encounter challenges and setbacks on the golf course, I look at them as opportunities to learn new skills and to become a stronger, more competent golfer.

Let's apply this golf discussion to marriage. Imagine a marriage in which the husband and wife think marriage is supposed to make them happy. They are miserable whenever conflicts and setbacks arise and may eventually want to walk away from the marriage altogether. Consider how differently this husband and wife would feel if they approached marriage with the focus of growing into more mature, agape-loving people who helped each other do the same. Each day would be an opportunity to learn something new about marriage and about each other. Each day would open the door for them to grow into more fully loving and wholehearted people. And, yes, both of them would be content, peaceful, and, dare I say it—happy—as a result.

Go back to the quote at the beginning of this chapter and mull it over for a moment. I'm not assuming Henry David Thoreau was referring to agape love when he said that we need to "turn [our] attention to other things." But I think he should have been. In this "all about me" world that worships at the altar of falling in love and feeling happy, we need to turn our attention to the highest kind of love—agape love. There is no more worthy "other thing" to turn our attention to. And if we turn our attention to loving our spouses this way, I believe being in love and feeling happy in marriage end up sitting softly on our shoulders.

PUTTING TRUTH INTO ACTION: DO THE FAIR THING

Acknowledge (believing this lie): "I believe that marriage is supposed to make me happy and that if I'm not happy, there is something seriously wrong with my marriage. I have made happiness an idol because I have made it more important than loving God, loving my spouse, and maturing into a full-fledged adult. I acknowledge that I think this way and that it is a lie."

In your own words, acknowledge believing this lie:

_____

_____

_____

_____

_____

_____

Assess (the cost of believing this lie): "Believing the lie that marriage is supposed to make me happy has led me to be bitter and resentful. It has led to getting caught up in self-medicating behavior in order to feel happy in the moment (eating, drinking, spending, lusting, and so on). It has caused me to treat my spouse unkindly, even cruelly at times, and resulted in me being difficult to be around. It has hindered my prayer life and closeness with God; it has caused me to be defensive when any of my flaws are pointed out; it has ..."

In your own words, assess the marital cost of believing this lie:

_____

_____

_____

_____

_____

_____

_____

Adopt (biblical truth):

"Until we all reach unity in the faith and in the knowledge of the Son of God and become mature, attaining to the whole measure of the fullness of Christ" (Eph. 4:13).

"Therefore let us go on toward perfection, leaving behind the basic teaching about Christ" (Heb. 6:1 NRSV).

"Let perseverance finish its work so that you may be mature and complete, not lacking anything" (James 1:4).

"But grow in the grace and knowledge of our Lord and Savior Jesus Christ" (2 Pet. 3:18).

Write down biblical truths that will help you defeat this lie:

_____

_____

_____

_____

_____

_____

Act (on truth): Come up with action steps you can take to facilitate your spouse's growth toward becoming a more complete person in Christ. For example, would it help your spouse to obtain more education, develop his or her talents and abilities, overcome a difficult struggle, or serve people in need? Identify what you can do to help make that happen so that you can help your spouse grow and mature.

In your own words, describe how you will put this truth into action:

_____

_____

_____

_____

_____

_____

Ask (for forgiveness): "Sweetheart, I wrongly believed that marriage was supposed to make me happy. Because of this belief I haven't treated you as lovingly and kindly as I should. I have treated you badly by _____ [refer to your list under **Assess**]. I want you to know I am working hard with God's help not to think or act this way anymore. Will you please forgive me for how I have treated you and pray that I will focus on helping you and me become the mature people God wants us to be?"

In your own words, ask your spouse to forgive you:

_____

_____

_____

_____

_____

_____

PRAYER

God, please help me to stop focusing on my happiness and to start focusing on helping me and my spouse mature. Please help me see the shortsightedness of seeking primarily happiness in marriage, and help me gain the farsightedness of understanding that the path to true joy lies in helping each of us grow. God, I'm sorry I have turned happiness into an idol in my marriage and ask You to help me repent of having done so. Please help me become more like Christ, the only fully mature and completely whole person to set foot on earth, and to help my spouse do the same. In the precious name of Jesus Christ and by the power of the Holy Spirit. Amen.

CHAPTER 3

YOU COMPLETE ME

Lie #2: My spouse can completely meet all my needs

*A marriage bound together by commitments to exploit the other
for filling one's own needs (and I fear that most marriages are
built on such a basis) can legitimately be described as a "tick on a
dog" relationship. Just as a hungry tick clamps on to a nourishing
host in anticipation of a meal, so each partner unites with the
other in the expectation of finding what his or her personal
nature demands. The rather frustrating dilemma, of course,
is that in such a marriage there are two ticks and no dog!*
—Larry Crabb, *The Marriage Builder*

*And my God will meet all your needs according
to the riches of his glory in Christ Jesus.*
—Philippians 4:19

In the movie *What about Bob?*, Bob Wiley is a comically troubled
man who has an extensive laundry list of psychological problems.[1]

Bob is referred to Dr. Leo Marvin, a pretentious psychiatrist whose
star is on the rise with the recent publication of his bestselling book,
Baby Steps. Bob is desperate for help with his problems, and he parasitically attaches himself to Dr. Marvin as being the one person on
the planet who can save him.

At the end of their first counseling session, Dr. Marvin tells Bob
he is going on a vacation with his family and will not be able to meet
for a month. Bob can't handle the thought of not seeing his psychiatrist for that long and has the gall to show up where Dr. Marvin is
vacationing with his family. Dr. Marvin is understandably miffed
that Bob didn't respect the boundary he drew, reminds Bob that he
is on a family vacation, and encourages Bob to go back home and
patiently wait for their next session. Bob, being the superneedy and
supermanipulative person he is, refuses to go away.

The two have a classic scene (I encourage you to watch it on
YouTube—it's pretty funny) in which Bob pleads with Dr. Marvin to
let him stay, saying, "Look, I'm in really bad shape, come on, please,
please, gimme, gimme, gimme. I need, I need, I need, I need, I need,
gimme, gimme, please!" Just to shut him up, Dr. Marvin foolishly
gives in to Bob's manipulative cries for help, sealing his own professional and personal fate in the process. Dr. Marvin tells Bob he can
stay, and Bob proceeds to turn his psychiatrist's life into a nightmare.

I mention this scene from *What about Bob?* because it points to
a lie that many of us believe about marriage. Bob believed that Dr.
Marvin could completely meet all his relationship needs and would
be his psychological savior. Like Bob with Dr. Marvin, many of us
believe our spouses are capable of meeting all our needs and can
psychologically save us. The truth is, they can't. Let's talk about our

relational needs for a few minutes and the lie that is woven into the fact that we have them.

THE LIE: MY SPOUSE CAN CATEGORICALLY, COMPLETELY, AND COMPREHENSIVELY MEET ALL MY NEEDS

Each of us is born with a God-wired longing for attachment. Our desire to bond with others is an essential aspect of who we are as human beings. Sometimes we get the message from the world we live in that wanting to be close to others is a sign of weakness, co-dependency, selfishness, or a shaky sense of self, and that if we aren't totally self-sufficient, something is seriously wrong with us. That's a bunch of nonsense. God didn't mess up when He made us long for connection and closeness with others.

Being able to achieve a healthy attachment with another human being is dependent on several factors, but one of the primary things is the willingness to meet each other's relational needs (you can also call them psychological needs, bonding needs, intimacy needs, or attachment needs). Some counselors might give you a list of sixty relational needs, while others might give you a list of six. In their workbook *Intimate Encounters*, Dr. David Ferguson and Teresa Ferguson suggest that our top-ten intimacy needs are acceptance, affection, appreciation, approval, attention, comfort, encouragement, respect, security, and support.[2] Quite a list, isn't it?

I believe we have these needs from the day we enter the world to the day we leave it. We are fundamentally needy in these ways our entire lives. If we aren't careful, we play into the Enemy's hands by believing we don't have these needs, believing we are selfish to have them, believing we can meet them all on our own, or believing we are entitled to others meeting those needs. But the truth is, you *do* have these relational needs, it is *not* selfish to have them, you *cannot* meet them all by yourself, and you are *not* entitled to your needs being met.

The biggest lie of all regarding psychological needs in marriage is this: "My spouse is supposed to fully meet each and every one of my needs and is falling down on the job if he [or she] doesn't." Embedded in this lie are two other deadly lies about marriage: (1) "My spouse is supposed to meet all my needs, but I don't have to meet all of my spouse's needs, especially the ones I don't want to meet"; and (2) "If my spouse doesn't meet my needs, I don't have to meet my spouse's needs." These three lies form the *unholy* trinity of faulty thinking about relational needs in marriage: "You are supposed to completely meet all my needs, I don't have to fully meet all your needs, and I don't have to meet your needs until you meet mine." Let me give you a quick snapshot of what each lie ends up looking like in a marriage.

In a "you are supposed to meet all my needs" marriage, both people feel let down by the other and end up feeling hurt and angry. Given that each person is expected to *fully and totally* meet the needs of the other, a task that is impossible to do, *neither spouse will feel that he or she is enough for the other.* The bar in these marriages is set so impossibly high that each day is just another painful reminder of what a complete and utter failure they are as mates.

In a "I don't have to meet all your needs" marriage, the spouses lose respect for each other because of the hypocrisy underneath:

demanding that your spouse meet all your needs while letting your-self off the hook for returning the favor. No one has much respect for a person whose attitude is "Do as I say, not as I do."

In a "I'm not going to meet your needs until you meet mine" marriage, the husband and wife end up in a paralyzing standoff of quid pro quo, each waiting for the other to be the first one to meet his or her needs. Airplanes are sometimes put in a holding pattern as they wait for a runway to open up for landing. This couple stays frozen in a withholding pattern, where each refuses to give anything to the other because the other person won't be the one to go first.

Over the years, I've counseled many couples who had spent their married lives fighting over this unholy trinity of lies, becoming more and more disconnected as the years passed by. If you don't want to end up that way, you have to embrace certain truths about having legitimate needs in marriage. Let's explore what they are.

... AND THE TRUTH ABOUT MARRIAGE WILL SET YOU FREE

Three critical truths come into play when it comes to our rela-tional needs in marriage. These can be difficult truths to apply, but with God's help we can get better at living them out in our marriages as the years pass by. I'll give you as much help as I can in learning how to apply these truths, then will trust that God will take it from there.

First, we must come to marriage "poor in spirit" (Matt. 5:3). When the Bible says, "Blessed are the poor in spirit," it doesn't mean we should take a vow of poverty or we are to have little in the way of material possessions. Being poor in spirit simply means that we are to acknowledge how deeply needy we are and that we lack the necessary resources inside ourselves for meeting our own needs. In marriage it means acknowledging we come to the table empty-handed, unable to meet our own relational needs.

To remind yourself to be "poor in spirit" in your marriage, I recommend that at least once a day, you ask God the following questions. First, "God, do I have relational needs in my marriage?" If you listen for God's voice, you will hear yes. Second, "God, is it okay to have these needs in my marriage?" If you listen for God's voice, you will hear yes. Third, "God, is it okay for me to want these needs to be met in my marriage?" If you listen for His voice, you will again hear God say yes. When you ask God these questions every day, you are inviting Him to help you become more "poor in spirit" over time in your marriage.

Second, we are to humbly and gratefully acknowledge that God is the one who "will meet all [our] needs according to the riches of his glory in Christ Jesus" (Phil. 4:19). God is the only one capable of fully meeting our needs. He is able to do so out of the abundance of being who He is (all-knowing, all-powerful, and everywhere at once). We are to turn to God as the one who can completely meet our needs, not our spouses or close friends or even counselors (I had to include that for the "Bobs" who go to counseling expecting their therapists to be their psychological saviors!). Because all of these people are fallen and finite, they can't come anywhere close to completely meeting our needs. At times they are even going to be the ones who wound us. But God will never let us down and will never wound us.

To apply this truth to your marriage, go to God with a particular need you have and ask Him to meet that need through your spouse. I think we can safely assume that God wants to work through your spouse to meet the legitimate needs you have. Then, take that need to your spouse and ask if he or she would be willing to meet it (rather than hope that in some supernatural, burning-bush kind of way, God somehow got the message across to your spouse without you having to bring it up). At that point, your spouse may allow God to work through him or her to meet that particular need. But if your spouse does not, look to God for how He will meet it in some other *legitimate* way (for example, prompting a same-sex friend to call you, meeting the need directly through the Holy Spirit inside you, using His Word to meet the need, and so on). I say "legitimate" here because I have actually met with clients who were having affairs and told me God had brought the people they were having affairs with into their lives in order to meet their intimacy needs. Believe me when I say that God will *never* meet your relational needs in sinful, illegitimate ways. Never.

Finally, we are to acknowledge that Christ "did not come to be served, but to serve" (Matt. 20:28). The idea here is that rather than go into marriage each day looking to take from our spouses, we need to be looking to give to our spouses. As Larry Crabb put it in the quote that opens this chapter, most marriages are "two ticks and no dog" in which each person is parasitically taking from the other. By contrast, isn't it mind-blowing to realize that God became a human being and served us? How incredibly humble of God to spend His short time on earth listening to us, healing us, encouraging us, washing our feet, treating us with respect, understanding us, and supporting us rather than demanding we do all of that for Him. His example is worth following.

The practical application of serving each other in marriage is difficult because in our "flesh" we are inherently bent toward taking, not giving. Our fallen selves rail at verses that say not to look "to [our] own interests" but "to the interests of the others" (Phil. 2:4), love "is not self-seeking" (1 Cor. 13:5), and "Let no debt remain outstanding, except the continuing debt to love one another" (Rom. 13:8). A lot of us are in a "two ticks and no dog" marriage in which we take so much more from each other than we give. Christ, the perfect role model for what it means to love, gave so much more than He ever received. It is extremely humbling to follow Christ's example, especially when your spouse doesn't seem to have any interest in doing so. Nevertheless, we are not to "become weary in doing good" (Gal. 6:9) but are to continue to "serve one another humbly in love" (Gal. 5:13).

I believe the Bible teaches this *holy trinity of truth* about our needs in marriage: I am *deeply* needy, God will *fully* meet my needs through all the various resources He has at His disposal, and I am to meet my spouse's needs as *best* I can whether my spouse meets my needs or not. Can you imagine taking these three attitudes into your marriage? How radically different would things be between you and your spouse if you did?

The title of this chapter is taken from a line in the movie *Jerry Maguire*.[3] "You complete me" is Hollywood movie-making nonsense. Another human being cannot complete you. The high level of neediness we bring into marriage is too much of a load to put on anyone's shoulders. Only someone who is truly "omni" can handle that kind of responsibility. We need to stop expecting our spouses to fully and completely meet our needs when only God is capable of doing that. Let's *lower* the bar to a more humane level when it comes to the needs we want our spouses to meet. Instead of *demanding* our spouses meet all our needs, let's *ask* them to meet the needs they can, genuinely appreciate it when they do, and watch in great anticipation as God meets all our needs through the people and means available to Him. Deal?

PUTTING TRUTH INTO ACTION: DO THE FAIR THING

Acknowledge (believing this lie): "I believed my spouse was capable of meeting all my relational needs, but I acknowledge this is a lie. I now know that no one person is capable of fully meeting all my needs and that it is wrong for me to pressure my spouse to do so. I acknowledge that only God is able to completely meet all my needs and that He will accomplish this through the wide variety of means at His disposal."

In your own words, acknowledge believing this lie:

_____

_____

_____

_____

_____

_____

Assess (the cost of believing this lie): "This lie has led me to demand that my spouse meet all my needs rather than turning to God for them to be met. I've put my spouse in the no-win situation of never being able to do enough to please me. I have been bitter and resentful toward my spouse for not meeting my needs and have treated my spouse in demeaning and devaluing ways. Because I have believed this lie, I have not expressed enough appreciation for the needs my spouse has met. I have created an environment in my marriage in which there is no joy in being in each other's presence. Rather than lovingly pursuing my spouse, I have withdrawn more and more. All of this is wrong and has created a toxic environment between the two of us."

In your own words, assess the marital cost of believing this lie:

_____

_____

_____

_____

_____

_____

_____

Adopt (biblical truth):

"And when you pray, do not keep on babbling like pagans, for they think they will be heard because of their many words. Do not be like them, for your Father knows what you need before you ask him" (Matt. 6:7–8).

"And my God will meet all your needs according to the riches of his glory in Christ Jesus" (Phil. 4:19).

"What is mankind that you are mindful of them, a son of man that you care for him?" (Heb. 2:6).

"Let us then approach God's throne of grace with confidence, so that we may receive mercy and find grace to help us in our time of need" (Heb. 4:16).

Write down biblical truths that will help you defeat this lie:

_____

_____

_____

_____

_____

_____

_____

Act (on truth): Given that we are supposed to follow the example of Christ and seek to serve others before ourselves, I encourage both of you to (1) create a list of needs, and then decide which two or three you would most like your spouse to meet; (2) share that list with your spouse; and (3) commit to asking God to help you meet those needs for each other. (I give additional action steps along these lines in chapter 12, so just focus on meeting your spouse's top two or three needs for now.)

In your own words, describe how you will put this truth into action:

_____

_____

_____

_____

_____

_____

_____

Ask (for forgiveness): "Sweetheart, I believed you should totally and completely meet all my needs, and I confess to you this lie. I have put pressure on you to meet all my needs and left you in a no-win situation. I have been bitter, resentful, and even mean toward you for not meeting all my needs, and I ask you to forgive me. I now understand the truth that I am to enter our marriage each day to serve, not to be served, and I want you to know I will work diligently to become that kind of spouse. Thank you for meeting my needs over the years. I will continue to try to meet as many of your needs as I can and will trust that God will use other appropriate people and means for fully meeting your needs each day."

In your own words, ask your spouse to forgive you:

_____

_____

_____

_____

PRAYER

God, please help me take my needs to You each day and be truly thankful for how You choose to meet them. Help me not to put my neediness on my spouse's shoulders, because it is simply too much of a load to carry. Help me see that You have a wide variety of ways to meet my spouse's needs and my own, and help me express genuine appreciation when my spouse meets my needs. Help me become the kind of person who thinks first about what my spouse needs from me, and help me gladly meet those needs. God, not only are You the provider of all I need, but You have gone well beyond my needs and given me so many of the things I desire in life. Thank You for being an extravagant God who gives me more than I could have ever hoped for or imagined. In the precious name of Jesus Christ and by the power of the Holy Spirit. Amen.

CHAPTER 4

THE PLANK IN YOUR EYE

Lie #3: My spouse is a bigger mess of a human being than I am

Never think you're better than anyone else,
but don't let anyone treat you like
you're worse than they are.
—Rip Torn, Actor

Do not think of yourself more highly than you ought.
—Romans 12:3

"Rebecca, you've got to stop spending so much. The amount we owe on our credit card is bigger than the national debt!"

"That's funny, sweetheart."

"I'm not laughing! I've been going through our credit card bill, and once again we don't have enough money to pay it off this month. We're getting hammered on the finance charges."

"You spend just as much as I do, Tom."

"I do not. I never get anything I don't need."

"Neither do I."

"Yes you do!"

"Give me an example!"

"Well, you spent a hundred dollars at the hair salon last week. Are you telling me that having your hair done costs a hundred dollars?"

"Yes, as a matter of fact, it does. And, remember, you're the one who didn't want me to let my hair go gray just yet."

"Well, it only costs me twenty bucks to get my hair cut, and that includes the tip."

"Get your hair colored, do you?"

"You don't need to be sarcastic about it."

"You're right. I'm sorry. But don't blame me that it costs a lot more for a woman to get her hair done than it does a man. By the way, can I see the credit card statement for a moment?"

"Why?"

"I just want to look at it for a second."

"I'm not sure why you want to look at it, but knock yourself out."

Tom handed Rebecca the statement, and after looking it over for a few minutes, she said, "What's this charge for ninety dollars at a golf course?"

"That's when I played golf with the guys from the office a couple of weeks ago."

"It costs ninety dollars to play golf? Isn't that a little high?"

"No, not if you want to play on a good course!"

"Do you have to play on a good course? Can't you play on a not-so-good course and save us some money?"

"Can't you let your hair go a little gray and save us some money?"

"If you want a wife who looks twenty years older than she is ..."

"You sure are snippy today."

In marriage there are things about our spouses that bug us, things they do or say that we dislike or disagree with. I'm talking here about small things, "marital misdemeanors," if you will. The problem is, even when our spouses have done only something minor, we can still end up flooded with emotions that, like a tsunami, hijack our minds and behavior, and make it almost impossible to think rationally and behave properly toward our spouses. In these moments of misdemeanor madness, a destructive lie comes into play, a lie that most of us would deny we believe. But believe it we do.

THE LIE: I'M A MUCH BETTER PERSON THAN YOU

In the dark comedy *The War of the Roses*,[1] the "I'm much better than you" attitude plays such a destructive role in one couple's marriage that (spoiler alert!) the husband and wife end up causing each other's demise. Oliver and Barbara Rose, two people who started out excited about the wonderful future they *thought* they were going to have together, end up battling so viciously over what each was going to get in their divorce settlement that they literally have a fight to the death.

Throughout the movie, the Roses do some pretty mean things to each other. Oliver cuts off the heels of his wife's expensive designer shoes, rudely disrupts an important dinner party she is hosting, and doesn't let her know he accidentally ran over and killed her beloved cat. Oliver does all of this because he thinks Barbara is a less-than-wonderful human being who loves her shoes, cooking, and cat more than she loves him (which, sadly, she does). Barbara traps Oliver in their in-home sauna until he passes out from heat dehydration, runs over his prized sports car *while he's in it*, and serves him pâté that, *after he eats it*, she implies may have been made from Oliver's much-beloved, missing dog. Barbara does all of this because she sees Oliver as a less-than-wonderful human being who loves his sauna, sports car, and dog more than he loves her (which, sadly, he does).

The War of the Roses does a painfully good job of portraying how husbands and wives can go from falling in love to feeling increasingly irritated by their spouses' quirks and flaws, to thinking they are superior to their spouses, to punishing their spouses for how they are. If you have never seen this movie or haven't seen it in a long time, I recommend you watch it as a couple. It is a powerful cautionary tale about just how badly things can go when you think you are better than your spouse.

Unfortunately, this dynamic happens all the time in marriage. After the glow of falling in love fades and we begin to see each other's warts more honestly, a lot of us think, *Oh, my gosh, what in the world have I gotten myself into? My spouse has all of these things wrong with him [or her]! How am I going to survive being married to this person?*

The cost of believing this lie is high. It keeps us from seeing our own shortcomings. It causes us to feel superior to our spouses and to think we are doing them a favor by continuing to be with them. And it leads to chronically "peering over the fence into your spouse's backyard" and critically pointing out all the weeds that are there.

Believing you are better than your spouse will cause you to act and speak in selfish ways. You will

- criticize your spouse's flaws,
- shame your spouse for having imperfections,
- become hypervigilant about looking for the next mistake your spouse makes,
- overlook the many positive qualities your spouse has,
- stiff-arm any effort on your spouse's part to point out your own imperfections, and
- walk around with a constant "smell" of superiority emanating from you and fouling the air.

In other words, believing this lie makes you a condescending and demeaning person, a person no one can feel close to.

Let me bring the Pharisees into this discussion for a second. The Pharisees were the poster children for people who thought they were better than everyone else. They constantly walked around with their noses up in the air about their self-righteousness and were always fouling the air with the stench of their moral superiority. I think it is important to note that the Pharisees were the group of people Christ was the most at odds with. It is also important to note that the Pharisees didn't end up in a close relationship with Christ and that I'm not reading into Scripture things that aren't there—they did not seem intimately close with *anyone*. They certainly weren't close to the people they looked down on, and they didn't even seem to be close to one another.

At this point, though, you may still want to argue, "But, Doc, I *am* a better person than my spouse! He [or she] has so many more flaws and shortcomings than I do it's not even funny!" If that's what you are thinking, I have a few thoughts for you.

... AND THE TRUTH ABOUT MARRIAGE WILL SET YOU FREE

I opened the chapter with Tom scolding his wife, Rebecca, about her spending habits. Tom let Rebecca know not only that he believed she sometimes spent more money than he thought was necessary (specifically, when she got her hair done) but also that he did not see himself as having any problem in that area of their marriage. Tom, whether he realized it or not, was treating Rebecca as though she was the flawed one in the marriage and he was a lot better than she.

You can tell from Rebecca's reaction that she didn't take too kindly to Tom's view of her as the only one who could be a little too free with spending money. That's why she asked for the credit card statement. She knew that Tom, being an imperfect human being, could also play a little too fast and loose with the greenbacks. She didn't have to scan the credit card bill too long before she saw that he had spent almost the same amount of money to play golf that she had spent to have her hair done. And she was more than glad to point that out. This was Rebecca's way of saying, "Hey, before you spend too much time in my backyard looking at what you think is wrong with me, you might want to take a look in your own backyard."

So, what do people who believe they are better than their spouses need to come to grips with before their marriages can be healthier and safer? Let me offer three truths I believe are required for you to stop thinking you are better than your spouse or, in other words, to "get over yourself."

First, there is nothing about your fallen self that is "good." The Bible clearly says that *all of us* come into the world with an inclination toward badness, which is referred to as the "flesh," or "sin nature." In talking about himself, here's what the apostle Paul had to say about our natural bent toward sin: "I know that good itself does not dwell in me, that is, in my sinful nature. For I have the desire to do what is good, but I cannot carry it out. For I do not do the good I want to do, but the evil I do not want to do—this I keep on doing" (Rom. 7:18–19). Paul understood, in a way that far too many Christians do not, that he had a natural bent toward sin—or a tendency to "miss the mark" of being righteous—and that his flesh was no darn good. Paul knew his sin nature tainted *everything* about him, not just certain areas of his life.

What I'm trying to emphasize is that you need to stop denying you are flawed across *every dimension of who you are.* There is nothing about you that your bent toward badness hasn't stained. Let me put it a different way: You need to get off your high horse and stop believing that there is anything about you that is perfectly good. There isn't. Christ ran into this attitude with the Pharisees. They thought pretty much everything about them was in great shape. Just the opposite was true—everything about them was flawed. If anything, Christ was trying to help them see they were probably *worse* than others because they thought they were *so much better*.

Second, you are not a better person than your spouse. I know it may bother some of you for me to say this, but it's true. Each of us comes into the world with a bent to do sinful things, so if you think you are a better person than your spouse, you're basically saying, "My badness isn't nearly as bad as my spouse's badness." Do you really want to argue that? I don't think so. Trust me, you don't want to get into a "who's better than whom" spitting contest with your spouse. I don't mean this rudely, but you smell just as bad as your spouse when it comes to the kind of human being you are, certainly in the nostrils of God.

You may not like this, but I need to say it: *even if you would never do the same grossly sinful thing your spouse has done (let's say, commit adultery), in your natural bent toward sin, you are capable of doing the same thing or have already done the equivalent.* Let me say that again so you won't just scoot right by it. If your spouse has committed a grievous wrong, a wrong that in your worst moment as a human being you would never see yourself committing, you are still no better than he or she is. Why? Because you are capable of doing exactly the same thing or have already done something as offensive. That's why God doesn't want you to compare yourself with your spouse. God wants you to compare yourself with the only truly good person who ever lived, Christ. Christ is the only true measuring stick for whether you are a good person. If you can muster the courage to compare yourself to Christ, you will never struggle again with thinking you are a good person or you are better than your spouse.

Third, humility is the most important character trait in marriage.
According to the Bible, humility is the main quality we are supposed to have in our interactions with others. There are too many
verses to cite, so let me give you just a few to consider: "All of you,
clothe yourselves with humility toward one another, because, 'God
opposes the proud but shows favor to the humble'" (1 Pet. 5:5); "Do
nothing out of selfish ambition or vain conceit. Rather, in humility value others above yourselves" (Phil. 2:3); "For those who exalt
themselves will be humbled, and those who humble themselves will
be exalted" (Matt. 23:12); "Remind the people to be subject to rulers
and authorities, to be obedient, to be ready to do whatever is good,
to slander no one, to be peaceable and considerate, and always to be
gentle toward everyone" (Titus 3:1–2). Humility is the numero uno
character trait we are supposed to allow God to develop in us.

I know I've said this before, but I have to say it again. Isn't it
amazing that God would take human form, much less be humble
in His interactions with us, while He was here? How humble it was
of Christ to wash our feet. How humble it was of Christ to listen to
us. How humble it was of Christ to attentively engage in discussion
with us. How humble it was of Christ to die on a cross for sins
we committed. I believe that the chief characteristic of Christ was
His humility, and the way He lived His life backed that up. Are
you beginning to understand why it is so offensive to God and to
your spouse that you "think of yourself more highly than you ought"
(Rom. 12:3) and walk around, as did the Pharisees, with your nose
up in the air?

If you want a healthy and thriving marriage, you need to do three
things: (1) turn away from the crazy notion that you are basically

good and turn toward the biblical view that your natural bent is to sin and "fall short of the glory of God" (Rom. 3:23), (2) accept that you are no better or worse than your spouse compared with Christ (Matt. 5:48), and (3) ask God to help you be humble (have an accurate sense of who you really are) when you interact with your mate (1 Pet. 5:5). It would be nice if we could snap our fingers and do all of this instantly, but it is a long and laborious process that we must "not grow weary" (Heb. 12:3) of working on.

Let's go back to Tom for a minute. He thought he was a good person in his spending habits ("I never get anything I don't need"), believed he was superior to Rebecca when it came to how he spent money ("*You've* got to stop spending so much"), and was proud about how he conducted himself in that area of their marriage (especially when he let her know he spent money only on "good" golf courses). These attitudes set the stage for him to jump the fence into Rebecca's backyard and start pointing out what he felt was wrong with her, a role he was never intended to have and one for which he was completely unqualified.

What if Tom had adopted the humble attitude I'm talking about in this chapter? Can you imagine how differently he would have responded to Rebecca if he truly believed (a) he was as bent toward doing wrong as she was, (b) he wasn't a better person than Rebecca compared with Christ, and (c) he needed God to help him eat a huge helping of humble pie every day? You don't have to be a psychologist to know Tom would have interacted in a completely different way with Rebecca. And you don't have to be a psychologist to know Rebecca would have responded to him in a much different way in return.

Your marriage will not be healthy and loving if you "fail to see the plank in your own eye" (Luke 6:42) while pointing out the "speck" in your spouse's eye. I wonder if the Bible refers to the flaws we see in others as a "speck of sawdust" but then refers to us as having a "plank" in our own eye because it is a much more grievous character defect to focus on the smaller things wrong with someone else than to ignore the bigger things wrong with ourselves (Matt. 7:3). I wonder if God is saying we use the misdemeanors our spouses commit to cover up or distract us from the felony we commit when we think we are better than our spouses. Hmm.

PUTTING TRUTH INTO ACTION: DO THE FAIR THING

Acknowledge (believing this lie): "God, even if only to a small degree, I believe I am an inherently good person and a better person than my spouse. I want to call these beliefs what they are: lies. Please help me quit thinking in such an arrogant and prideful manner. Help me admit I have a natural bent toward doing wrong and that I am no better than my spouse in how I'm living my life compared with Christ."

In your own words, acknowledge believing this lie:

_____

_____

_____

_____

_____

Assess (the cost of believing this lie): "Believing I am a better person than my spouse has caused me to treat my spouse in demeaning, shaming, and denigrating ways. Specifically, I have been overly critical, rarely expressing words of affirmation to my spouse, and I have reacted punitively when my spouse has done something wrong. I have withheld forgiveness and have pulled away into self-righteous aloneness. I have not been kind, gracious, or humble in interacting with my spouse, and I have sinfully driven a wounding wedge between the two of us."

In your own words, assess the marital cost of believing this lie:

_____

_____

_____

_____

_____

_____

_____

_____

Adopt (biblical truth):

"Where there is strife, there is pride" (Prov. 13:10).

"You hypocrite, first take the plank out of your own eye, and then you will see clearly to remove the speck from your brother's eye" (Matt. 7:5).

"For all have sinned and fall short of the glory of God" (Rom. 3:23).

"For I know that good itself does not dwell in me, that is, in my sinful nature" (Rom. 7:18).

"Do nothing out of selfish ambition or vain conceit. Rather, in humility value others above yourselves" (Phil. 2:3).

"Humble yourselves before the Lord, and he will lift you up" (James 4:10).

Write down biblical truths that will help you defeat this lie:

_____

_____

_____

_____

_____

_____

_____

Act (on truth): The fastest path to becoming a humble person is to emulate Christ; He "did not come to be served, but to serve" (Matt. 20:28). So, go to your spouse and ask how you can serve him or her. If your spouse's request is appropriate (meaning, as long as your spouse doesn't ask you to do something immoral, unethical, or impossible), meet the request. The bottom line here is to look for ways to "wash your spouse's feet."

In your own words, describe how you will put this truth into action:

_____

_____

_____

_____

_____

_____

_____

Ask (for forgiveness): "Sweetheart, I have bought into the lie that I am better than you. I know I am not. I want to apologize to you for being so arrogant and ask you to forgive me for _____ [spell out the specific ways you have acted as though you're better than your spouse]. Please pray that I will increasingly see both of us as fellow strugglers with feet of clay, two people who fall far short of being like Christ, and that I would humbly work on my owns flaws in our marriage and not try to work on yours."

In your own words, ask your spouse to forgive you:

_____

_____

_____

_____

_____

_____

_____

PRAYER

God, how incredible it is that You are the Creator of the universe, yet You are humble in spirit. How amazing it is that You are perfectly holy, yet have no pride or arrogance in You. When You look at my many flaws and imperfections, it is not in a condemning or shaming manner, and You never lord Your greatness over me. Help me stop being so full of myself that I think I am better than my spouse. Help me practice humility consistently so that I interact with my spouse in a loving and gracious manner. Forgive me for believing I am more like You than I am like my spouse. How arrogant of me! I am nothing like You and everything like my spouse. Help me remember this every day I live. In the precious name of Jesus Christ and by the power of the Holy Spirit. Amen.

CHAPTER 5

I'M THE KING (OR QUEEN) OF THE WORLD

Lie #4: I am entitled to my spouse's love

I'm here today to warn you: I want you
to watch out for the adversary.
Guard yourself from any spirit of entitlement.
—Charles R. Swindoll

He mocks proud mockers but shows favor to the humble.
—Proverbs 3:34

"Pete, I know you're at work right now, but would you pick up the kids from school this afternoon?"

"Melanie, I don't have time to pick them up. I've got a meeting with my boss at three."

"Well, I don't have the time either, and *I* dropped them off this morning."

"What does dropping the kids off this morning have to do with me picking them up this afternoon?"

"I just thought it would be a nice thing for you to do given that I'm the one who always carts them around."

"Melanie, that's part of *your* job! That's what you're supposed to do! I'm not against helping you out when I can, but you sound like you think I owe it to you!"

"Well, that's how you act when you come home. You seem to think that after working hard all day you deserve to come home to a meal on the table, a clean house, and the kids all taken care of."

"After I've worked hard all day, I *do* come home expecting you to have done all the things you're supposed to do. I don't think that's unreasonable."

"Look, if you don't want to help me out, just say so."

"It's not that I don't want to help you out! I can't help you out! And I resent you laying a guilt trip on me like I'm doing something wrong!"

"Pete, I'm not laying a guilt trip on you. I just said it would be nice if you would help me out with the kids once in a while."

"Oh, so I never help you out with the kids. Look, don't call me at work again unless you have a genuine emergency on your hands."

"I didn't know the kids and I have to be dying to call and ask you for help!"

Hidden in the deepest recesses of our minds is a lie that is accepted as a self-evident truth in our world today. Consequently, a lot of us grow up being told not only that it is the right way to think, but also that no one should ever question or disagree with us about it. When this lie rears its ugly head in marriage, it leads to conflict that never seems to get resolved and a husband and a wife feeling bitter and resentful. Let's put on our mental spelunking gear and see what this lie is all about.

THE LIE: I'M ENTITLED TO WHAT I WANT FROM MY SPOUSE

We live in a world that tells us we are *entitled* to things in life. The largest fast-food company in the world tells us we "*deserve* a break today," and one of the world's largest retailers declares, "*Expect* more. Pay less." Motivational speakers tell us to "never settle for anything less than you *deserve*" and to "*demand* the very best." Everywhere we turn, we are told we are entitled to things—we should demand having things our way, expect people to give us what we want when we want it, and believe we are owed nothing less.

At the risk of you throwing this book across the room, I want to tell you that all of those ideas are godless nonsense and will irreparably damage your marriage if you believe them. If you go into your marriage believing that you are entitled to things from your spouse (love, kindness, fairness, honesty, openness, support, help, sex, a break from the kids, a hall pass on getting your work done each day, a romantic weekend in the South of France, and so on), you are ensuring that your relationship will be an unpleasant, unsafe, and unstable place, and that the two of you will have a hard time ever feeling close. Let me explain.

At least two things can happen when you feel entitled to your spouse giving you what you want. One is that he or she actually *gives it to you*. Let's say Cathy, a talented and hardworking lawyer, comes home from a long day at work and *expects* her husband, Sam, an underemployed part-time sales associate at a local electronics store, to have dinner ready. When Cathy walks into the house, she sees that Sam has, in fact, gotten dinner ready. Given that Cathy felt *entitled* and that she *expected* Sam to do this, all that rattles around in her mind is, *Well, that's what he was supposed to do.* She doesn't thank Sam or feel any appreciation for his effort to make her life easier when she comes home from work—even though he worked that day too. Consequently, the most flattering emotion Cathy experiences toward Sam for making dinner is selfish satisfaction.

The second thing that can happen is he or she *doesn't give it to you*. Let's say Cathy comes home from an especially grueling day at work, expecting Sam to have dinner ready. Not only has he not gotten dinner ready, but Sam is playing "Assassinate and Annihilate," a wildly popular video game, on their superexpensive flat-screen television that he bought using Cathy's year-end bonus check. Sam, giddy over having just made his highest score ever, shares his excitement with Cathy. How do you think she will respond?

You don't have to be a marital therapist to know that Cathy is going to feel bitter and resentful toward her husband. And since she believes that Sam's failure to prepare dinner is what made her feel this way, she's likely to pay him back in some hurtful manner (options include throwing "Assassinate and Annihilate" in the trash, not speaking to him for the rest of the night, slamming cabinet doors in the kitchen while she makes dinner, and withholding sex).

When I think of a person in Scripture whose life illustrates just how bad things can go in a marriage and a family when one person feels entitled, I think of David, the shepherd-king. While the Bible doesn't say David felt entitled, I think it is a reasonable assumption based on what it does tell us about him.

On the upside, David was a talented musician (1 Sam. 16:23), a world-class poet (he authored many of the psalms), a highly successful military leader (1 Sam. 18:7), a wildly popular king (1 Sam. 16–2 Sam. 24), as good-looking as Brad Pitt (1 Sam. 16:12), brave and skillful enough to have killed wild animals and a nine-foot-tall Philistine when he was just a boy (1 Sam. 17:34–35, 50), well-spoken (1 Sam. 16:18), a man after God's own heart (1 Sam. 13:14), and in the generational line of Jesus Christ (Matt. 1:6). If ever there was a person who was "the best of the best of the best," it was David.

On the downside, David had multiple wives and concubines (1 Sam. 18–2 Sam. 11), committed adultery with Bathsheba (2 Sam. 11:4), had Bathsheba's husband killed in battle to cover up their sin (2 Sam. 11:14–15), brought calamity on his family and country because he slept with Bathsheba (2 Sam. 12:11–12), and was an underinvolved father who did not properly discipline his children (2 Sam. 13). If ever there was a person with significant character flaws, it was David.

For the purposes of this chapter, I want to zero in on David's sin with Bathsheba. Before I do, I want you to know I am not doing so with an attitude of superiority toward David. None of us, and that certainly includes me, come anywhere close to being the kind of person God wants us to be. All of us have significant character defects as we go through life, and those defects seriously wound God and the people we love. All of us live in glass houses, so I want you to know I am not throwing stones at David with what I'm about to say.

I have three questions about David. First, how could a man with numerous wives and concubines take a married woman he didn't even know into his bedroom when all his sexual needs were, theoretically, already being met? Second, how could he, after finding out Bathsheba was pregnant with his child, orchestrate having her husband killed in battle to cover it up? Third, how could he—when he had been blessed by God with so many incredible personal traits and abilities, had achieved world-shaping levels of success, and had everything he could ever want—do such horrible things?

I could be wrong about this, but I wonder if David had grown to feel entitled to have whatever he wanted whenever he wanted it. I wonder if he had begun to believe his own press clippings. Had he come to feel entitled because of who he was and all the things he had accomplished? Had he fallen into thinking that the rules of righteous behavior no longer applied to him because he was so special? Even though he was a man after God's own heart, had David become so prideful and complacent in his relationship with God that his sexual passions got the best of him? Was it his sense of entitlement that brought David down? I don't know for sure, but I think this may have very well been the case.

David's life was never the same after his sin with Bathsheba. His family fell apart, he deeply mourned the death of the child he had with Bathsheba, and one of his sons drove him out of power. We have to give David some credit, though, because he didn't flinch when

Nathan confronted him about his adultery with Bathsheba. David acknowledged his sin, was truly sorry about what he had done, was able to claim God's grace and forgiveness, and returned as the king of Israel (2 Sam. 12).

Here are some things we can take away from David's life. First, all of us can fall into thinking we are entitled to what we want in life. Second, all of us can feel we deserve pleasurable payback for possessing unique personal qualities and achieving great success. Third, all of us can allow our relationship with God to atrophy to such a dangerously low level that we are more susceptible to indulging sinful forms of self-soothing (alcoholism, drug addiction, adultery, overeating, overspending, and so on). And, fourth, all of us can get to the point where we run straight off the edge of the entitlement cliff to our own destruction and to the destruction of those around us, a cliff that had Thou Shalt Not warning signs posted all over it.

Entitlement is a primary source of conflict in couples who come in for marriage counseling. It isn't uncommon for husbands and wives to feel entitled to having what they want from their spouses and to resent it when their spouses don't comply. That was the case for Melanie and Pete, the couple from the opening of this chapter. Melanie felt she was entitled to Pete picking up the kids that afternoon because she was the one who "always cart[ed] them around." Pete, after a hard day at work, felt entitled to come home to a hot meal, a clean home, and well-behaved kids. As a result of their feelings of entitlement, neither of them genuinely appreciated the positive things the other did and resented it when the other didn't do what was expected.

So, if we are not entitled to what we want from our spouses, what are we supposed to think? To answer that question, I'd like to compare the shepherd-king, David, with the King of Kings, Christ.

… AND THE TRUTH ABOUT MARRIAGE WILL SET YOU FREE

While David had many wonderful qualities and achieved great things, Christ, being God in human form, was a million times more intelligent, wise, discerning, courageous, powerful, gifted, strong, and moral. In leaving heaven, Christ gave up His status and privilege and "made himself nothing" here on earth (Phil. 2:7). He denied himself on earth. And, yet, in a way that ought to fry our mental circuits, *Christ never felt entitled to anything.*

Christ never once felt people *owed* Him anything for meeting their needs, never once demanded people meet His needs, never once felt entitled to being treated like a king, never once expected people to respond lovingly to Him after He had been loving to them, and never once said He deserved to be treated better than He was treated. God came to earth in the form of a man and didn't expect red-carpet treatment even though He was the Creator of the universe. Christ never felt He "deserved a break today." Christ didn't subscribe to the slogan "Expect more. Pay less." Christ never "demanded the very best" in terms of what He got out of life. And because Christ never felt entitled to anything, He was truly grateful and appreciative when people treated Him well and never felt bitter or resentful when they treated Him badly. And, man, did they treat Him badly.

Having the attitude of Christ in marriage means you under-stand this: *you are not now nor will you ever be entitled to anything from your spouse.* This means do not think you are entitled to your spouse being loving, kind, thoughtful, supportive, fair, sexual, responsible, hardworking, giving, loyal, attentive, or anything else. It means you understand having positive attributes or great successes doesn't make you entitled to having a spouse who is everything you want him or her to be or who does everything you want. It means you understand you do not deserve payback for anything or from anyone.

Christ was God in human form, but He didn't arrive on the planet feeling as if He was owed anything. This is the very planet He created, and we are the very people He knit together in our mothers' wombs (Ps. 139:13). But Christ was laid in a feeding trough after He was born (Luke 2:7), had to be taken to Egypt so Herod's assassins wouldn't murder Him (Matt. 2:13), had no place to lay His head (Luke 9:58), and was treated like the lowest of the lows while He was here (Luke 22–23). In light of all of this, can you understand why it is so offensive to God when we feel entitled to things from Him or from other human beings? If Christ, who was God, humbled Himself enough *not* to feel entitled to things, is it much of a leap to assume God sees us as being arrogant when we think we are entitled to anything?

I think God's aversion to this sense of entitlement is partly why He responded the way He did to Job's questions and complaints. Sure, Job was unfairly stripped of all the people he loved, all his posses-sions, his physical health, and certainly his peace of mind. Job had every reason to feel angry, hurt, sad, and dismayed, especially given he was "blameless and upright" and "he feared God and shunned evil" (Job 1:1). But Job's righteousness and fear of God didn't entitle him to being protected from all these bad things happening. So after Job complained about his situation and even questioned God's character because of it, God graciously and truthfully brought the hammer down when He said, "Who is this that obscures my plans with words without knowledge? Brace yourself like a man; I will question you, and you shall answer me. Where were you when I laid the earth's foundation? Tell me, if you understand" (Job 38:2–4). God made it crystal clear that Job was not entitled to anything here on earth.

In the book of Job, I think God is trying to help all of us see that no matter who we are, no matter what we have accomplished, no matter how moral we are, no matter what wonderful qualities we possess, and no matter what good or bad comes our way, we are not entitled to anything. I think God is also telling all of us who question His character and His motives that He does not *owe* us an explanation for why there are "the righteous who get what the wicked deserve, and the wicked who get what the righteous deserve" (Eccles. 8:14). A word to the wise: please don't ever think you are entitled to anything from God or that you can question His character. God, as He did with Job and as He did with David, loves you enough that He will take you out behind the proverbial woodshed and give you the "foster your growth spanking" you so richly deserve because "the Lord disciplines the one he loves" (Heb. 12:6). I've gotten that spanking from God more than a few dozen times, and I can tell you it is not a lot of fun.

We need to give Job some credit, though. After God put him in his place about not being the one who "laid the earth's foundation,"

Job came to his senses and said, "I know that you can do all things; no purpose of yours can be thwarted. You asked, 'Who is this that obscures my plans without knowledge?' Surely I spoke of things I did not understand, things too wonderful for me to know" (Job 42:2–3). Job reacquainted himself with the fact that there is one God and it wasn't him. He reacquainted himself with the fact that God's character and motives are always good and never to be questioned. I find it interesting that after Job came to his senses, God "blessed the latter part of Job's life more than the former part" (Job 42:12), and he died "an old man and full of years" (Job 42:17). Job wasn't owed a better life than what he had before, but wasn't it rather tender and kind of God to give one to him?

I want to say one final thing about what it means to repent of having an attitude of entitlement in your marriage. Or, should I say, what it doesn't mean. Letting go of feeling you are entitled doesn't mean you let go of *wanting or desiring* things from your spouse. It is perfectly appropriate to want or desire your spouse to meet your spiritual, emotional, sexual, and financial needs in marriage and to feel disappointed, sad, hurt, and frustrated when he or she doesn't. Let's go back to the life of Christ to understand this.

While Christ never felt entitled to anything from others, at times He put His needs in play and hoped they would be met. For example, when His soul was "overwhelmed with sorrow to the point of death" about the cross that awaited Him, Christ told His disciples to "stay … and keep watch" while He went off to pray (Mark 14:34). After He finished praying, Christ came back "and found them sleeping" (Mark 14:37). We might say that Christ put His relational need for support in front of His disciples that day. I may be projecting my own human emotions onto Christ in all of this, but I sense hurt, sadness, and even frustration in His words when He asked these men, men whom He had been pouring His heart and soul into for three years, "Couldn't you keep watch for one hour?" (Mark 14:37). Nevertheless, because Christ didn't feel entitled to their support, He wasn't bitter or resentful toward His disciples after they fell asleep when He needed them most.

Can you imagine having the mind of Christ with regard to not feeling entitled to anything? Can you see how free from bitterness you would be? Can you imagine being in a marriage in which you don't feel entitled to anything from your spouse? Can you see how free you would be from resentment toward your mate? Can you imagine how not feeling bitter or resentful toward your spouse would free you to respond in a loving manner when your spouse doesn't give you what you want?

If you want your marriage to thrive, you must learn to express your needs without feeling entitled to your spouse meeting them. In the days and weeks to come, instead of saying to your spouse, "I *expect* more time and attention from you than I've been getting," say, "Would you be willing to spend more time with me?" Instead of saying, "I *deserve* help with the kids," say, "It would mean a lot to me if you would give me more help with the kids." Instead of saying, "I'm *entitled* to being treated better by you," say, "I would appreciate it if you would talk to me in a more respectful manner." Remember, there is a right way to express your needs to your spouse and to express the hurt and anger you feel when your spouse does not meet them.

I want to challenge you to make a decision *right now* to drop your attitude of entitlement in your marriage and to adopt an attitude of humility. Instead of demanding, humbly ask your spouse to meet your needs. If all of us could do this one simple thing—to humbly present our wants and needs to our spouses in a "you don't owe me" manner—they will feel more inspired to give us everything we could have ever hoped for or imagined.

PUTTING TRUTH INTO ACTION: DO THE FAIR THING

Acknowledge (believing this lie): "I believe I am entitled to what I want from my spouse. But that is a lie; I am not. I believe I am owed what I want from my spouse. But that is a lie; I am not. I expect my spouse to give me what I want. But that is wrong. I demand my spouse meet my needs, and that is wrong."

In your own words, acknowledge believing this lie:

_____

_____

_____

_____

_____

_____

_____

Assess (the cost of believing this lie): "Believing I am entitled to what I want from my spouse has led me to be bitter, resentful, and punitive. I have held on to my resentment and have not forgiven my spouse for failing to meet my needs. I have taken out my bitterness on my spouse by pulling away at times and being blatantly hostile at other times. I have created a marriage in which it is not okay for my spouse to be unwilling to meet my needs and have reacted with contempt when that happens. Because I feel entitled to what I want from my spouse, I have not been grateful or appreciative when given what I expect."

In your own words, assess the marital cost of believing this lie:

_____

_____

_____

_____

_____

_____

Adopt (biblical truth):

"The LORD sends poverty and wealth; he humbles and he exalts" (1 Sam. 2:7).

"He guides the humble in what is right and teaches them his way" (Ps. 25:9).

"He mocks proud mockers but shows favor to the humble and oppressed" (Prov. 3:34).

"Take my yoke upon you and learn from me, for I am gentle and humble in heart" (Matt. 11:29).

"Be completely humble and gentle; be patient, bearing with one another in love" (Eph. 4:2).

"Humble yourselves, therefore, under God's mighty hand, that he may lift you up in due time" (1 Pet. 5:6).

Write down biblical truths that will help you defeat this lie:

_____

_____

_____

_____

_____

_____

Act (on truth): Start having meetings with your spouse in which you both express your needs, wants, and desires. Use that time to humbly ask your spouse to meet these needs, but reassure your spouse that if he or she chooses not to meet them, you will respond in a loving, respectful manner. If your spouse does meet your needs, show genuine appreciation and gratitude.

In your own words, describe how you will put truth into action:

_____

_____

_____

_____

_____

_____

_____

_____

Ask (for forgiveness): "I apologize for thinking I deserve to get what I want from you, to have expected you to give me what I want, to have demanded you give me what I want, and to have ever felt owed anything in return for what I have done for you. Please forgive me and pray that I will love you with no strings attached and not think I am owed anything in return."

In your own words, ask your spouse to forgive you:

_____

_____

_____

_____

_____

_____

_____

PRAYER

God, how truly amazing it is that You are the Creator of the universe and yet are humble. How incredible it is that You give so much to us but don't feel owed anything in return. God, I know You long for us to love You with all our hearts, souls, and minds, yet You are so humble and pour out Your love and blessings on us with no expectation of us responding in kind. Please help me be more like You, completely humble in spirit. Help me realize that even though I desire love from my spouse, I am to expect nothing from my spouse, that my spouse owes me nothing, and that I am entitled to nothing. Help me see things that way so that when my spouse gives me what I want, I am filled with genuine gratitude and appreciation and express both. In the precious name of Jesus Christ and by the power of the Holy Spirit. Amen.

CHAPTER 6

IT TAKES TWO TO TANGO

Lie #5: Our marital problems are all my spouse's fault

A man can fail many times, but he isn't a failure
until he begins to blame somebody else.

—John Burroughs, American Naturalist

"Have you eaten from the tree that I commanded you not
to eat from?" The man said, "The woman you put here with
me—she gave me some fruit from the tree, and I ate it." Then
the LORD God said to the woman, "What is this you have done?"
The woman said, "The serpent deceived me, and I ate."

—Genesis 3:11–13

In the romantic comedy *Mr. and Mrs. Smith*,[1] a man and a woman fall in love and marry, unaware that they are both world-class assassins employed by competing murder-for-hire agencies (yes, this is a romantic comedy). After being sent by their respective agencies to kill the same person, John and Jane Smith discover they are in the same profession but are competitors. Understandably, both are angry that the other has lied throughout the marriage about his or her line of work (and, as it turns out, everything else they have ever told each other about their backgrounds).

The agencies John and Jane work for won't allow them to stay married, so they are ordered to tell the other to either leave town or be killed. Given that both are married to their jobs more than each other and are hurt and angry about having been deceived over the years, neither will leave town. So each tries to take the other's life in an effort to eliminate the competition in the murder-for-hire world (yes, once again, this is a romantic comedy).

Jane thinks she killed John by blowing up the steel cables to an elevator and sending him hurtling down sixty floors to his death (he was actually in a different elevator at the time she blew up the cables). After thinking she killed him, Jane goes to the restaurant where John proposed to her in order to console herself, because she did actually love him (however slightly). John tracks her there, they exchange unpleasantries, and he asks Jane to dance (mainly so he can frisk her for weapons, just in case she still wants to kill him). At one point during their dance, the following exchange takes place:

Jane: Why is it you think we failed? Because we were leading separate lives, or was it all the lying that did us in?

John: I have a theory ... newly formed.

Jane: I'm breathless to hear it.

John: *You* killed us. *You* approached our marriage like a job,
           something to be reconned, planned and executed.

Jane: And *you* avoided it.²

In this chapter, I want to focus on a lie that is common in "Mr.
and Mrs. Smith" types of marriages. This particular lie goes all the
way back to the garden of Eden, when Eve blamed the serpent for
her choice to take a bite out of a piece of fruit and Adam blamed
his wife and the God who gave her to him for doing the same thing
(Gen. 3:11–13). On that day this lie shattered everything about
our relationship with God and our relationships with other human
beings, and we haven't been right since.

Before you read the next section, you need to know that you
believe this lie more deeply than you realize, that it is an incredibly
destructive way to think, and that this lie is killing any chance you
and your spouse have of developing a loving marriage. It is such a
toxic way to think that if you continue to believe it, your marriage
can't help dying a very slow and painful death.

THE LIE: IT'S YOUR FAULT OUR MARRIAGE ISN'T GOING WELL ... AND, WHILE WE'RE ON THE SUBJECT, YOU'RE ALSO TO BLAME FOR WHY I TREAT YOU THE WAY I DO

In *The Road Less Traveled*,³ M. Scott Peck wrote that people make
two mistakes when it comes to taking responsibility. One mistake
is to *take too much* responsibility. When you act this way, we psychologist types say you are being "neurotic" because you're taking

responsibility for things you are not actually responsible for. The other mistake is to *take too little* responsibility. When you act this way, we say you are "character disordered" because you're not taking responsibility for the things you are actually responsible for.

Let's apply this to marriage. I know this may sound wrong, even unbiblical, but you are being neurotic when you take responsibility for your spouse's feelings and behavior ("It's my fault my spouse is unhappy and spends money like there's no tomorrow"). I know your more neurotic side is going to have a hard time hearing this, but *you're not responsible for how your spouse feels or acts; your spouse is.* On the other hand, you are being character disordered when you blame your spouse for how you feel and act ("It's my spouse's fault I'm unhappy and spend money like there's no tomorrow"). I know your more character-disordered side is going to have a hard time hearing this, but *your spouse is not responsible for how you feel and act; you are.*

In most marriages, spouses bounce back and forth like a pin ball between being neurotic and being character disordered, and this is one of the reasons a lot of couples can't resolve conflict. How can you resolve conflict if one or both of you vacillate between taking too much and too little responsibility concerning the issue at hand? You can't. That's why Satan likes us to fall into either mistake—he knows that we will stay at odds with each other and that an endless number of suns will go down on our anger. Ephesians 4:26–27 says, "'In your anger do not sin': Do not let the sun go down while you are still angry, and do not give the devil a foothold."

I believe the bigger of these two mistakes occurs when we take too little responsibility. While it certainly isn't healthy to take too much responsibility, those who chronically blame their feelings and

actions on their spouses are the more intractable group and are causing the greater amount of damage. These marriage partners have a
much greater tendency to deny the "plank" in their own eye and are
rarely genuinely sorry for the bad things they do (Matt. 7:3). As a
psychologist, I find it easier to help a person stop taking too much
responsibility than it is to help someone take more.

Let me give you an example of what this "neurotic versus character disordered" dynamic looks like in marriage. Let's say that Harold
forgot Maude's birthday. Maude is *deeply* hurt and angry that Harold
forgot her birthday and reads him the riot act for doing so. Maude,
giving in to her more character-disordered side, blames Harold for
the hurt and anger she feels, for her decision to tear up their wedding
pictures, and for throwing all his clothes in the backyard. How is
Harold to respond to all of this?

If Harold is a *neurotic* husband, he will take Maude's verbal and
emotional abuse and see himself as responsible for causing her to feel
and act this way. "Sweetheart, it's my fault you're feeling hurt and
angry. After all, I was the one who forgot your birthday. It's my fault
you tore up our wedding pictures, and I have only myself to blame
that you threw my clothes out in the backyard. It was only right that
I spent the night sleeping with the dogs in the doghouse in freezing
weather." Sadly, Harold is taking responsibility not only for forgetting his wife's birthday (which he is responsible for), but also for how
Maude responded to him.

If Harold is a *character-disordered* spouse, he will abusively fire
back at Maude, blaming her for making him angry at how she's treating him for forgetting her birthday. He will blame Maude not only
for making him mad but also for making him throw all her *Downton*

Abbey DVDs in the front yard. "Sweetheart, you're hacking me off by being such a witch about me forgetting your birthday, and it's your fault I threw all your precious *Downton Abbey* DVDs in the flower bed." Here, not only is Harold refusing to take responsibility for forgetting his wife's birthday, but he is also blaming her for how he reacted to her mistreatment.

Now, if Harold is going to be a responsible husband in this marriage, here is how he should handle forgetting Maude's birthday: "Sweetheart, I am truly sorry I forgot your birthday. It was my fault, and I was wrong. I understand that you feel hurt and angry about it. Will you forgive me?"

Now at this point, if Maude is going to "woman up," she should say, "Sweetheart, of course I forgive you. Thanks for apologizing and asking for forgiveness. I want to ask you to forgive me for treating you like I did. You didn't deserve to be treated that way, and it was wrong of me. Will you forgive me for blaming you for my anger, throwing your clothes in the backyard, and making you sleep in the cold with the dogs?"

Finally, if Harold wants to put a nice cherry on top of this particular marital interaction, he should say, "Yes, of course I forgive you. Thanks for apologizing. Can I make all of this up to you by taking you out to celebrate your birthday?" Maude then says, "Thanks for the offer—that would mean a lot to me." And off they go to enjoy marital life, liberty, and the pursuit of happiness.

None of this can happen if a spouse believes the lie that "our marital problems are your fault, and you are to blame for how I treat you." Such a marital relationship is headed toward ever-increasing mistrust, fear, and even hostility. This particular attitude guarantees that a husband and wife will not be able to resolve the conflict they are having and won't be able to come back together in a loving and safe manner. That's why the "father of lies" wants couples to think this way.

So what's the truth about who is responsible for how well or poorly a marriage is doing? Who is responsible for the "state of the union"?

... AND THE TRUTH ABOUT MARRIAGE WILL SET YOU FREE

The truth of the matter is that *both of you* are responsible for the state of your marriage, regardless of who committed the offense of the moment or any offenses in the past. Let me explain.

Marriage is a "it takes two to tango" relationship in which both of you contribute, for better or for worse, to the overall health or sickness of the relationship. Think of yourselves as a mixed-doubles team in tennis. If you were to get beaten by an opponent, you wouldn't blame your partner for the loss, would you? (You wouldn't, right? Promise me you wouldn't do that.) In order for your partner to have been the sole reason for the loss, every ball in the match would have to have been hit only to your spouse, who then didn't make any returns. This would mean you couldn't—or didn't—even participate.

I played a lot of tennis growing up, and I can promise you that *you win or lose as a team.* Even when your partner is having an off day and missing more shots than you are, how well or poorly you played was a collective effort. It is just flat-out wrong to go up to your doubles partner after a loss and say, "It's your fault we lost. You're a horrible tennis player, and I am never going to play tennis with you again!" If you understand the game of tennis, you would never do that. And if you truly understand the "game" of marriage, you would never do that. Metaphorically, both people in a marriage struggle to get the ball back over the net, and, with few exceptions, most people choose spouses or playing partners who are at their same basic skill level. If you won or lost today as a couple in terms of how you got along, you are both responsible.

A number of important biblical truths come into play with this lie of believing your marital problems are your spouse's fault and your spouse is to blame for how you treat him or her. Let me zero in on just one.

The Bible is clear that a day is coming when we all are going to stand before God and give an account of our actions. Paul said, "You, then, why do you judge your brother or sister? Or why do you treat them with contempt? For we will all stand before God's judgment seat. It is written: 'As surely as I live,' says the Lord, 'every knee will bow before me; every tongue will acknowledge God.' So then, each of us will give an account of ourselves to God" (Rom. 14:10–12). I'm no theological scholar, but I'm pretty sure this is saying that we are responsible for our own actions while we're here and that a time is coming when blaming others for how we feel and how we act is going to come to a screeching halt. I wonder if the most important implication of this verse is in how we conduct ourselves in marriage.

Apparently, God isn't going to let you stand in His presence at the end of your life and say, "It was my spouse's fault we had a difficult marriage, and, furthermore, any bad behavior I displayed toward my spouse was also my spouse's fault!" I don't think any of us want to have that much chutzpah before God when our lives are finally over. That God allows us to do as much blaming and scapegoating as we do here on earth is a testimony to just how gracious, patient, and long-suffering He is toward us.

But notice what the Bible *isn't* saying here. It isn't saying you are going to give an account for your spouse's actions. *God doesn't hold you accountable for your spouse's feelings and actions.* So if your spouse blames you for how he or she feels or acts, I believe God gives you permission to say, "I want you to know I care very deeply about how you feel. With all due respect, though, I'm not going to take responsibility for how you feel or how you act in our marriage. We are each responsible for what we feel and how we act. Let's work on having that kind of marriage together, okay?"

Let's turn again to the life of Christ and take a look at how He approached taking responsibility in His interactions with others.

First, Christ never blamed Himself for what others felt or did. He never said things like, "It was My fault Judas betrayed Me" or "I'm to blame for Peter denying knowing Me" or "It's My fault the Pharisees hated Me and plotted to have Me killed." Christ was never neurotic in His interactions with others. He held people completely responsible for how they felt and how they acted.

Second, Christ never blamed His feelings and actions on others. He never said things like, "It was the money lenders' fault I got angry and drove them out of the temple that day" or "It was the Pharisees' fault I called them a bunch of hypocrites" or "You horrible sinners are to blame for why I died on a cross." Christ was never character disordered in His interactions with others. He took complete responsibility for His feelings and for His actions.

If you want to have a healthy, loving marriage, you have to stop blaming your spouse for how you feel and how you act and you must stop allowing your spouse to blame you for how he or she feels and acts. Two important steps come into play when taking appropriate responsibility in marriage.

First, you have to switch from "you" language to "I" language. Try to discipline yourself to stop saying, "You made me mad" or "You're the reason I stormed out of the house." Say instead, "I feel angry about what you did …" or "I chose to storm out of the house." It may sound like semantics, but you are not going to stop blaming your spouse for your feelings and actions until you start using the word *I* rather than *you* in marriage.

Second, when you blame your feelings or actions on your spouse, make sure you apologize and ask for his or her forgiveness. It should sound something like this: "I blamed you earlier for how angry I was and for yelling at you. I apologize for doing that and ask for your forgiveness. You are not to blame for how I feel or how I act in our marriage, and I am truly sorry I said you were. Will you forgive me?"

Human history has been marked by people taking far too little responsibility for their own feelings and actions. Consequently, people have tended toward being character disordered. It is interesting, though, that one of the most common sayings in recent years has been, "When you point one finger at me, you're pointing three back at you." At some level, people seem to at least intellectually understand that people who blame others for their emotions and actions are running away from taking responsibility for their own stuff. Nevertheless, finger-pointing continues on a grand scale in our world today, and it seems to be especially common in marriage.

If you are going to let the truth set you free in your marriage, you can no longer blame your spouse for how the marriage is going or for how you feel or act. And you can no longer accept blame for how the marriage is going and for how your spouse feels or acts. For a marriage to be truly healthy, both people have to think the way Christ did about the issue of responsibility. Christ knew that every one of His relationships was "cocreated" in that both people played into how things were going. (Of course, given that Christ was perfect, He had the luxury of knowing that if a relationship with someone was going *badly*, it truly was *all that person's fault.*) Also, Christ didn't blame others for how He felt and acted, and He didn't allow others to blame Him for how they felt and acted. It's that simple. Both of you need to take joint responsibility for how the marriage is doing and sole responsibility for how you feel and act toward each other.

Hebrews 4:13 says, "Nothing in all creation is hidden from God's sight. Everything is uncovered and laid bare before the eyes of him to whom we must give account." We are going to stand before God someday and give an account of what we thought, felt, and did. Whatever else we need to *stop* doing in marriage, we need to stop playing the "blame your feelings and actions on your spouse" game. And whatever else we need to *start* doing in marriage, we need to start playing the "own your own feelings and actions" game.

The apostle Paul said, "When I was a child, I talked liked a child, I thought like a child, I reasoned like a child. When I became a man, I put the ways of childhood behind me" (1 Cor. 13:11). When we are children, we have a tendency to think in neurotic ways ("It's my fault the teacher yelled at me because I was talking in class") and in character-disordered ways ("It's the teacher's fault I left my homework at school"). We can't help thinking *both* ways when we are young, so we need to extend our "when I was a child" selves a lot of grace on this. But if, as adults, we are still thinking both ways, we haven't put childish ways behind us. While we need to extend grace to ourselves, we also need to face the fact that we haven't fully entered adulthood yet, that it is costing our marriages dearly, and that we need to turn from it.

The bottom line is you can't have a loving marriage if you think like a neurotic child ("It's my fault my spouse is angry") or a character-disordered child ("It's my spouse's fault I'm angry"). Childish ways of thinking won't help you have an adult relationship with your spouse. We need God to help us stop blaming our stuff on our spouses and help us stop taking the blame for our spouses' stuff. We don't need to keep thinking the faulty ways we did when we were six. We can grow up. The choice is ours.

PUTTING TRUTH INTO ACTION: DO THE FAIR THING

Acknowledge (believing this lie): "It is embarrassing to admit, but I find myself blaming my spouse for the problems we have in our marriage and for how I have treated my spouse over the years. I acknowledge that both of these ways of thinking are wrong. It is a lie to think my spouse is the only reason we don't get along, and it is also a lie to think my spouse is to blame for how I act."

In your own words, acknowledge believing this lie:

_____

_____

_____

_____

_____

_____

Assess (the cost of this lie): "Believing my spouse is to blame for the problems in our marriage has led me to be critical, cold, condemning, and condescending. I have walked around in the marriage acting superior and have behaved as if there is nothing wrong with me. Blaming my spouse for our marital struggles has led me to be a difficult and wounding person and has resulted in a marriage in which my spouse does not feel safe to be around me. I have played a significant role in creating a marriage in which it isn't okay to be a flawed human being and in which I blame my spouse for everything that's wrong with us."

In your own words, assess the marital cost of believing this lie:

_____

_____

_____

_____

_____

Adopt (biblical truth):

"Now we know that whatever the law says, it says to those who are under the law, so that every mouth may be silenced and the whole world held accountable to God" (Rom. 3:19).

"So then, each of us will give an account of ourselves to God" (Rom. 14:12).

"Nothing in all creation is hidden from God's sight. Everything is uncovered and laid bare before the eyes of him to whom we must give account" (Heb. 4:13).

Write down biblical truths that will help you defeat this lie:

_____

_____

_____

_____

_____

_____

_____

Act (on truth): I discussed this earlier, but I want you to put this truth into action in three different ways. First, I want you to learn to use the word *I* instead of *you* when you are talking to your spouse. Instead of saying, "You made me mad when you ate the last piece of cheesecake," say, "I felt angry when I realized you ate the last piece of cheesecake." Second, I want you to apologize to your spouse when you blame him or her for how you feel or act and to ask for forgiveness. Third, I want you to appropriately stand up to your spouse when your spouse blames you for his or her actions. Instead of saying, "You can't blame me anymore for your feelings and actions because Dr. Thurman said so," say, "Sweetheart, I would greatly appreciate it if you would stop blaming me for how you feel or act. I want to understand how you felt about what I did; I just don't want you to blame me for how you felt. Can we agree to that?"

In your own words, describe how you will put this truth into action:

_____

_____

_____

_____

_____

_____

_____

Ask (for forgiveness): "I have blamed you over the years for the problems in our marriage, and I am sorry. I have also blamed you for how I have acted toward you, and I apologize for that as well. I have not taken responsibility for my part in why we struggle as a couple, and it is wrong and immature of me to blame you for how I have acted. I am working hard on taking responsibility for my own part in how our marriage is doing, and I am going to work equally hard on taking full responsibility for how I treat you day to day. I hope you will forgive me for blaming you for our problems and for my wrong behavior, and I hope you will pray for me as I try to become more like the spouse God wants me to be."

In your own words, ask your spouse to forgive you:

_____

_____

_____

_____

_____

_____

_____

PRAYER

God, too much of my marital life has been spent blaming my spouse for how I feel and how I act. I am truly sorry I have been this way and have fallen into the bitterness and resentment that go along with it. Thank You for showing us in the life of Christ what it looks like when a person takes responsibility for his or her actions. Help me to stop blaming my spouse and to start taking responsibility for my contribution to the problems we have in our marriage and for the way I treat my spouse. Help me humble myself in front of my spouse as an equally flawed human being who needs as much grace and forgiveness as anyone. In the precious name of Jesus Christ and by the power of the Holy Spirit. Amen.

CHAPTER 7

I YAM WHO I YAM

Lie #6: My spouse should accept me just the way I am

"Be yourself" is about the worst advice you can give some people.
—Thomas Lansing Masson

If you really change your ways and your actions and deal with each other justly, if you do not oppress the foreigner, the fatherless or the widow and do not shed innocent blood in this place, and if you do not follow other gods to your own harm, then I will let you live in this place, in the land I gave your ancestors for ever and ever.
—Jeremiah 7:5–7

"Blake, would you *please* put your dishes in the dishwasher after you eat! You always leave them in the sink!"

"First of all, I don't *always* leave my dishes in the sink. And, second, why are you making such a big deal about it?"

"I'm not making a big deal out of it! I'm just not going to keep putting your dishes in the dishwasher like I'm your maid!"

"Then don't! Stop putting my dirty dishes away, and please get off my back about it!"

"What am I supposed to do, just leave them there? Look, you're not single anymore ... Our home isn't your bachelor pad where you can leave things wherever you want! Leaving your dishes in the sink really irritates me ... not that you care."

"Patty, I care ... I just think you're *way* too obsessive and controlling about how the kitchen looks."

"Well, we obviously have completely different standards for what it means to keep the kitchen clean ... and, if I left it up to you, you'd never put a dirty dish away."

"Why do you have to make everything worse than it really is? Can't you ever make your point without being overly dramatic?"

"I'm not being overly dramatic! I just think you don't see how inconsiderate you are! *I'm not going to clean up after you anymore!*"

"Fine! Leave my dishes alone, and I'll take care of them when I'm good and ready!"

"So, you *don't* really care about how I feel about it, do you?"

"I'm done with this conversation. I'm going on a run."

"Fine, go do your own thing—it's what you're really good at!"

In marriage, a lot of battles take place between a husband and wife. One of the biggest is over the changes that each wants *the other to make.* Needless to say, most of us don't take too kindly to our mates telling us what's wrong with us, much less demanding we change.

For many of us, when our spouses criticize us about our faults and demand that we change, "Them's fighting words."

In this chapter, I want to explore the lie underneath the fights that couples have over the flaws they bring into marriage, a lie that leaves a husband and wife in a relationship in which personal growth and development are unlikely and genuine reconciliation is infrequent. Very few of us realize that we think this way or acknowledge just how destructive this lie is to marital peace and harmony. Let's lift the hood on this lie and see how it prevents the marital engine from running smoothly.

THE LIE: YOU NEED TO ACCEPT ME AS I AM, AND NEVER, UNDER ANY CIRCUMSTANCES, ASK ME TO CHANGE

Growing up, I loved watching cartoons. Every Saturday morning was pure bliss because I got to watch cartoons to my heart's content. It didn't matter which cartoon was on because I liked them all. Some of my personal favorites were *Top Cat*, *The Rocky and Bullwinkle Show*, *The Road Runner Show*, *The Jetsons*, *Clutch Cargo*, *The Flintstones*, *The Yogi Bear Show*, *Mighty Mouse* … I could go on and on and on. Ah, those were the days!

But how can you talk about your favorite cartoon shows without mentioning *Popeye the Sailor*? *Popeye the Sailor* was, in my humble opinion, one of the best cartoons of all time. It was like Lay's potato chips—you couldn't watch just one episode; you had to watch twenty.

Many iconic lines came from *Popeye the Sailor*. My personal favorite is "I yam what I yam." I don't know for sure what Popeye meant by this, but I think he was saying, "Look, what you see is what you get. I'm okay with who I am, and you need to accept that this is who I am always going to be." If Popeye had a favorite song, it probably would have been "I've Gotta Be Me" ("I gotta be me, I've gotta be me, what else can I be but what I am?"[1]). So what does all of this have to do with the chapter we're in? I'm glad you asked.

A fair number of husbands and wives have a "Popeye attitude" in their marriages. They have the mind-set of "I am who I am, I accept how I am, and you need to deal with the fact that this is who I'm always going to be" and resent it when their spouses point out that everything about them isn't all peaches and cream. When these husbands and wives hear their spouses say, "Hey, I don't like this about you, and I think you need to change," they get defensive, start circling the wagons around their flaws, and become angry at their spouses for having the nerve to challenge them about their more irksome qualities.

In my practice I run into a lot of husbands and wives who want their spouses to stop nagging them about their flaws and give them what humanistic psychologists call "unconditional positive regard." The fundamental premise of unconditional positive regard, a concept developed by psychologist Carl Rogers in the 1960s, is that people need to be accepted and valued regardless of how they are acting.[2] In giving others unconditional positive regard, we are supposed to set aside all our values, opinions, and judgments, and provide a safe environment for them to talk about their struggles without any fear of being challenged or criticized. Rogers believed if people receive unconditional acceptance, they will not only talk more openly and honestly about their issues but will also have the internal resources to make positive changes in the direction of personal growth and development.

As nice as that sounds in theory, I don't think that unconditional positive regard is a biblical concept or that it fosters growth and development in human relationships. It especially doesn't help a marriage improve. Let me explain.

Yes, we are to accept our spouses as they are (Rom. 15:7: "Accept one another, then, just as Christ accepted you, in order to bring praise to God"), be gracious and humble in how we interact with our mates (Col. 4:6: "Let your conversation be always full of grace"; Eph. 4:2: "Be completely humble and gentle"), avoid being judgmental and condemning toward our husbands or wives about their flaws and defects (Matt. 7:1: "Do not judge, or you too will be judged"; Rom. 8:1: "There is now no condemnation for those who are in Christ Jesus"), and provide a safe environment in which our spouses can be free from fear when they share their most difficult and troubling struggles (1 John 4:18: "Perfect love drives out fear"). We are to offer all of these components of unconditional positive regard to our spouses.

However, Scripture also tells us to speak "the truth in love" (Eph. 4:15) when we see that someone is headed off in an unhealthy and destructive direction, to "go and point out [his or her] fault, just between the two of you" (Matt. 18:15) when someone does something wrong, and to remember that "better is open rebuke than hidden love" (Prov. 27:5) when a person has acted badly and won't own up to doing so. Unconditional positive regard ignores these biblical teachings. It leaves out the side of love that involves caring enough about someone to confront and challenge that person to turn and go in a healthy direction when he or she is out of line.

All of this reminds me of the work of another humanistic psychotherapist, Dr. Frederick (Fritz) Perls. Perls penned the popular Gestalt Prayer in the late 1960s (posters of the prayer seemed to be everywhere you looked back then, and you still run into them today), and it was a perfect fit for the individualism of the "me generation" of baby boomers growing up during that time. Part of the Gestalt Prayer points out that we are not in this world to live up to other people's expectations and that "I do my thing and you do your thing."[3]

Yes, it's true: we are not in this world to live up to other people's expectations, and other people are not in this world to live up to ours. But I think the deadly part of the Gestalt Prayer is "I do my thing and you do your thing." Just like the notion of unconditional positive regard, that idea sounds nice in theory, but it doesn't work in human relationships. It especially won't fly in marriage. What if "doing your thing" means being selfish, abusive, unfaithful, lazy, or irresponsible in your marriage? Is your spouse supposed to bathe those things about you in unconditional positive regard and say, "Hey, no big deal; you're just doing your thing"? I don't think so.

So let's bring Popeye, Perls, and Rogers all together to see what this attitude looks like in a lot of today's marriages: "I am who I am; you need to accept me as I am; you need to positively regard me no matter how I act; you need to accept that I'm always going to be this way, whether you like it or not; and if you don't like the way I am, feel free to leave." The last three statements are *especially* deadly to your marriage being a healthy and safe place: "You need to positively regard me no matter how I act," "You need to accept that I'm always going to be this way," and "If you don't like the way I am, feel free to leave."

Blake and Patty, the couple I opened the chapter with, had this attitude in their marriage, much to their own detriment. Blake wanted Patty to give him unconditional positive regard for leaving his dirty dishes in the sink and for avoiding conflict by going out for a run. Patty wanted Blake to give her unconditional positive regard for being obsessive and controlling about keeping the kitchen clean and for being critical that he didn't share her standards. Consequently, things weren't going well for them.

Notice how things played out between this couple. Blake, angry about Patty getting on him about leaving dirty dishes in the sink and pointing out he was no longer a bachelor, shut everything down by saying he was "done with this conversation" and going on a run. Patty, angry that Blake was defensively holding on to his way of doing things, sarcastically told him that doing his own thing was what he was "really good at." When the dust had settled from their fight, Blake and Patty weren't going to reach a place of mutual understanding, much less reconciliation, unless both of them changed. Only then would they be able to come to an agreement on how things were going to be done in their marriage.

So if we are who we are, if we aren't here to live up to our spouses' expectations, and if we are free to do our own thing whether our spouses like it or not, what is our attitude supposed to be about a spouse who has flaws and defects that lead us to want to scream and pull out our hair? How are we supposed to interact with our spouses when their peccadilloes trigger such strong reactions?

... AND THE TRUTH ABOUT MARRIAGE WILL SET YOU FREE

While I am aware that what I'm about to say falls into the "easier said than done" category of marriage, here is the truth of the matter. We are supposed to interact with our spouses about their flaws the way Christ interacted with people about their flaws: "full of grace and truth" (John 1:14). Let me do the best I can to explain that.

First, Christ was "full of grace." Although I can't say I completely understand what this means, I know I have experienced God's grace. Perhaps it means Christ was kind, caring, empathic, courteous, civil, tenderhearted, and accepting toward everyone He encountered. And even when He strongly rebuked people, Christ was no less caring and good-hearted in His interactions with them. Christ was gracious to every person He met, and it didn't matter who the person was, what problems he or she was having, or how well or badly the person was acting. Christ was full of grace whether the person was male or female, Jew or Gentile, wealthy or poor, healthy or sick, moral or immoral, strong or weak, arrogant or humble, appreciative or ungrateful, kind or mean, deep or shallow, real or fake. Christ completely accepted and fully valued everyone He met. To borrow a line from the Billy Joel song "Just the Way You Are,"[4] Christ would have had no problem singing, "I love you just the way you are" to everyone He encountered.

Second, Christ was "full of truth." Again, I don't pretend to understand all that this means either, but I believe that part of what it means is that Christ saw people exactly as they really were.

He never saw people as being better than they were, and He never saw them as being worse than they were. Consequently, when Christ held up a mirror for people to see themselves, His mirror was free from distortion. Christ spoke "the truth, the whole truth, and nothing but the truth" to people when He gave them input. To tweak the Billy Joel lyric just a little, Christ would have had no problem singing, "I *see* you just the way you are."

Here are a couple of examples for your consideration. On the positive side, when Christ encountered a Roman centurion whose servant was sick, and said, "Truly I tell you, I have not found anyone in Israel with such great faith" (Matt. 8:10), He was being accurate and honest about this man. The Roman centurion had such great faith that he told Christ, "Just say the word, and my servant will be healed" (Matt. 8:8). On the negative side, when Christ called the Pharisees "hypocrites" and "whitewashed tombs" (Matt. 23:27), He was being accurate and honest about them. The Pharisees were a bunch of self-righteous hypocrites who didn't practice what they preached. Christ saw this about them and called them on it. He always told it as it was to people when He addressed their strengths and weaknesses.

Obviously, none of us come anywhere close to being like Christ in how we interact with our husbands or wives. Nevertheless, we are to make every effort to be "full of grace and truth" when we talk to our spouses, especially when we are telling them we think they need to change. We are to be gracious in that we are to be kind, caring, civil, empathic, understanding, considerate, tender, and humble. We are to be truthful in that we are to be as honest, accurate, proportional, reality based, and free from distortion as we can be. For our marriages to be truly Christian, we have to offer both grace and truth to our spouses. We simply cannot afford to speak truth if there is no grace behind our words, and we cannot afford to be gracious if there is no truth behind what we say.

To drive this grace-and-truth discussion home, let's take a quick look at how Christ interacted with the woman caught in adultery. Was Christ "full of grace" about her living a sexually immoral life? Yes, He was. Christ's graciousness toward her was expressed when He said, "Then neither do I condemn you" (John 8:11). Was Christ "full of truth" about her living a sexually immoral life? Yes, He was. Christ's truthfulness to her was expressed when He said, "Go now and leave your life of sin" (John 8:11). Christ was fully gracious and fully truthful with this woman, and my guess is that she had never gotten both from one person before and that she never got over getting both from one person.

The painful part of marriage for many of us is how often we feel that our spouses' feedback about our flaws lacks both grace and truth. Sadly, many husbands and wives have so much anger and resentment toward each other that when they finally say something about their partners' flaws, it is unkind (mean, hateful, shaming) and inaccurate (distorted, disproportional, and untrue). As Aristotle so eloquently put it, "Anyone can become angry—that is easy, but to be angry with the right person at the right time, and for the right purpose and in the right way—that is not within everyone's power and that is not easy."[5] When it comes to marriage, we sometimes feel our spouses go after our faults at the wrong time, for the wrong purpose, and in the wrong way. Is it any wonder we shut conversations down so quickly and go on a run?

It is important to understand that marriage is about the tender and the tough sides of love. It is about being gracious, but it is also about being truthful. Whether we like it or not, God wants to use our spouses as mouthpieces to address our rough edges, those *seemingly* small things about us that are bothersome and even wounding to our spouses. God can't do that if all we want from our spouses is for them to "get off our backs" and bathe us in unconditional positive regard.

So, please, listen to what your spouse says you need to change about yourself. It may well be from God Himself. And even if your spouse says things about you at the wrong time, in the wrong way, and with the wrong motive, try to be man or woman enough to listen for the part that is true and to allow God to polish that particular rough edge off how you "do your thing." *Seek* your spouse's input on your flaws and defects. Say, "Sweetheart, I would like to know what you think I need to change because I want to be a better spouse to you as the years pass by." It'll totally freak your spouse out! If *both* of you would be willing to do that, over time not only will you become a better "I yam what I yam," but your marriage will also become a better "We yam what we yam."

PUTTING TRUTH INTO ACTION: DO THE FAIR THING

Acknowledge (believing this lie): "I have bought into the notion that my spouse should accept everything about me, give me nothing but unconditional positive regard about who I am, and never push me to make any changes in how I act. I acknowledge this is a deadly way of thinking about marriage that doesn't line up with the attitude God wants me to have."

In your own words, acknowledge believing this lie:

_____

_____

_____

_____

_____

_____

_____

Assess (the cost of believing this lie): "Believing this lie has led me to be defensive when my spouse confronts me regarding inappropriate behavior on my part. Instead of welcoming and valuing my spouse's input, I have responded bitterly and resentfully. This has cost me the respect of my spouse. I have reacted as if my spouse is wrong and has nothing to offer in helping me see myself as I really am. My attitude has caused us to drift further and further apart. It has filled our relationship with tension, frustration, and anger instead of the tenderness and warmth we both long for."

In your own words, assess the marital cost of believing this lie:

_____

_____

_____

_____

_____

_____

Adopt (biblical truth):

"Better is open rebuke than hidden love" (Prov. 27:5).

"Wounds from a friend can be trusted, but an enemy multiples kisses" (Prov. 27:6).

"As iron sharpens iron, so one person sharpens another" (Prov. 27:17).

"If your brother or sister sins, go and point out their fault, just between the two of you" (Matt. 18:15).

"Instead, speaking the truth in love, we will grow to become in every respect the mature body of him who is the head, that is, Christ" (Eph. 4:15).

Write down biblical truths that will help you defeat this lie:

_____

_____

_____

_____

_____

_____

_____

Act (on truth): One way you could act on this truth is to set aside one time each week to ask for your spouse's input. Ask each other,

"What would you like me to work on this week that would leave you feeling safer and more loved?" Another way you could act on this truth is to write down flaws that have already been brought to your attention and then ask each other, "Which of these would you like to see me work on changing first?" Then, get someone other than your spouse to hold you accountable for making that change.

In your own words, describe how you will put this truth into action:

_____

_____

_____

_____

_____

_____

_____

Ask (for forgiveness): "I have refused to acknowledge I have things to work on, and I have remained the same person I was when you married me. I am sorry I have demanded you accept me as I am without giving you any room to ever challenge me to change. Will you please forgive me for this and pray that I will become the person God wants me to be?"

In your own words, ask your spouse to forgive you:

_____

_____

_____

_____

_____

_____

_____

PRAYER

God, I have been defensive about my flaws and have reacted badly when my spouse points them out. I have refused to allow You to work through my spouse to help me see the things I need to change, dishonoring You and my mate in the process. Help me listen when my spouse speaks the truth in love to me. Help me graciously receive my spouse's feedback about my flaws—rather than get defensive or angry—and prayerfully bring that feedback to You. Even if my spouse confronts me unlovingly, help me be willing to see if what my spouse says is true. And, if it is, give me the courage and strength to change. God, please help me become the kind of spouse who seeks corrective feedback rather than runs away from it. Help me become the kind of person my spouse would never be afraid to lovingly challenge or confront. In the precious name of Jesus Christ and by the power of the Holy Spirit. Amen.

CHAPTER 8

OPPOSITES
~~ATTRACT~~ ANNOY

Lie #7: My spouse should be just like me

We are the sun and moon, dear friend; we are sea and land.
It is not our purpose to become each other; it is to recognize
each other, to learn to see the other and honor him for
what he is: each the other's opposite and complement.
—Hermann Hesse, *Narcissus and Goldmund*

For you created my inmost being; you knit me
together in my mother's womb. I praise you because
I am fearfully and wonderfully made; your works
are wonderful, I know that full well.
—Psalm 139:13–14

"Sweetheart, I would appreciate it if you wouldn't leave your jogging shoes by the side of the bed. They smell bad and I trip over them all the time," Brenda tells Chuck as they pull out of their garage on the way to a restaurant and movie for their date night.

"That's where I like to put them," he responds.

"Well, it would mean a lot to me if you would start putting them in your closet."

"I'll think about it. By the way, I would really appreciate it if you wouldn't leave dirty dishes in the sink after dinner."

"But I like to do the dinner dishes right before I go to bed!"

"That's all well and good, but the roaches are really enjoying the seven-course meal they get every evening."

"I forget how funny you are. Can we talk about something else?"

"What else do you want to talk about?"

"Well, I also wanted to ask if you would stop turning the thermostat down so low before we go to bed. I'm freezing to death every night and having trouble falling asleep."

"Well, I'm burning up every night and can't fall asleep either."

"I guess I'll just have to buy more blankets."

"We don't need any more blankets. Can't you go a single day without buying something?"

"Let's just go on home. I can tell this isn't going to be a very enjoyable evening."

"Fine with me ... I don't like Italian food and didn't want to go to the restaurant you picked out, anyway!"

"Well, I didn't want to see the movie you picked out ... Can we ever go to a movie that doesn't involve things blowing up and cars crashing into each other?"

"I like action movies. Unlike you, I don't need to see movies where everyone cries all the time."

In the previous chapter, I mentioned that a lot of battles go on in a marriage, and I homed in on the battle over things that each spouse would like to see the other change, *things that actually need to change.* In this chapter, the focus is on a much different battle, one that doesn't have anything to do with a husband or a wife needing to change anything about who he or she is. This battle is about being different.

In every marriage, spouses have some things in common, but they also have ways in which they differ. Sometimes the differences are rather large, large as in polar opposites of each other. Opposites may very well attract, but a lot of people then don't really like that their partners are so different. That can lead to criticizing each other's differences. As psychologist Charles Lowery put it, "Opposites attract, but after marriage, opposites attack."[1] Let's explore the destructive lie underneath a husband and wife criticizing each other simply for being different.

THE LIE: YOU SHOULD THINK, FEEL, AND ACT JUST AS I DO, AND YOU'RE WEIRD, ODD, OR STRANGE IF YOU DON'T!

"You should be exactly like me" is one of the biggest lies I continue to struggle with in my relationship with Holly. I came into our marriage with very definite ideas (some might say rigid, but they obviously don't know what they are talking about). I thought I knew the "right way" to do things, and I believed Holly was wrong if she didn't do things my way. Let me give you just a small sampling of how I used to think things should be done around our house. If a movie were made of all of this (starring either Brad Pitt or George Clooney, of course), it would be titled *The World According to Chris*. Here are the rules I believed our household should live by:

- Toilet paper should be hung with the sheet coming *over the top* so you can easily find it when you need it.
- Never leave the front or back door open because God doesn't want us to air-condition the neighborhood.
- Set the thermostat such that you are uncomfortable—your discomfort is far less important than the fact that we are saving money on our utility bill.
- Cover the sofa and chairs in the family room with sheets so that when you take them off, it doesn't look as if human beings actually sit there.
- *Never* eat in a carpeted area of the house.
- Do not allow black, green, or white stuff to build up in the shower.
- Never leave lights on in a room if you are not in it.

- Load a dishwasher for maximum space utilization—
  no open spaces.
- Push your chair back under the table when you
  are done sitting there.
- Never leave your stuff in a place you aren't; put it
  where it belongs.
- Comply with all of these rules because this is *the
  right way to do things.*

I'm a fairly obsessive-compulsive, controlling, and perfectionistic person, so I am not the easiest person on the planet to live with. Since Holly doesn't share my need to have everything perfectly and obsessive-compulsively ordered and controlled, we've had hundreds of clashes over how our ways of doing things are so very different.

Now where would I get the idea that Holly should be like me in how she thinks, feels, and acts? Where does the "you should be just like me and you're wrong when you aren't" attitude come from? Well, let me suggest that it comes from inside ourselves, like Narcissus, who saw his own reflection in a pool one day and fell in love with it.

We don't have time to go into an in-depth exploration of what narcissism is or what causes someone to be this way (and, to be honest, I'm not well-studied enough on this issue to be able to do that for you). I believe narcissism is an important issue for all of us to learn more about because we all struggle with it to a certain degree, especially in our interactions with our spouses. That being said, let me mention some of the criteria we counselor types use to diagnose narcissistic personality disorder. The individual

- has a grandiose sense of self-importance;
- believes he or she is "special" and unique and can be understood by, or should associate with, only other special or high-status people;
- requires excessive admiration;
- has a sense of entitlement;
- is interpersonally exploitative;
- lacks empathy—is unwilling to recognize or identify with the feelings and needs of others; and
- shows arrogant, haughty behaviors or attitudes.[2]

Sound like anyone you know? (No, I'm not talking about your spouse.) What I'm suggesting here is that the belief that our spouses should be just like us is a reflection of how narcissistic we can be. Though only a small percentage of the population actually is diagnosed with this personality disorder, many of us fall into the trap of being egocentric—having thoughts about how grandiose we are ("My ways are so much better than yours"), how special we think we are ("Do you know just how lucky you are to have me?"), how much admiration we require from others ("You should worship the ground I walk on"), how entitled we think we are to people doing things our way ("I expect you to do things the way I want them done"), how lacking in empathy we can be about what it is like to live with us ("You've got a lot of nerve to feel hurt and angry toward me!"), and how arrogant we can be toward our spouses ("Your way of doing things is inferior to mine"). When it comes to our self-centered sides in marriage, our favorite hymn isn't "How Great *Thou* Art";[3] it's "How Great *I* Art." And while narcissism is woven into every one of the lies examined in this book, in some way it especially shows itself in the demand that our spouses mirror our greatness back to us by being exactly like us.

Unfortunately, Chuck and Brenda, the couple I introduced at the beginning of this chapter, were revealing their narcissistic sides in their interactions with each other. Both had a fairly critical attitude toward the other about their differences and thought their own particular ways of being were superior to their spouse's. Brenda didn't like that Chuck left his running shoes by his bedside (too smelly), how low he set the thermostat (too cold), and that he enjoyed action films in which things get blown up and cars crash (too violent). Chuck didn't like that Brenda waited until bedtime to do the dinner dishes (too late), how high she set the thermostat (too hot), that she enjoyed Italian food (too rich), and that she loved films in which people cry (too sad). Sadly, Chuck and Brenda had long forgotten what they did like about each other. They were semipermanently camped out on all the things they didn't like and how they thought the other should be their clone.

So what are husbands and wives supposed to do if they believe their ways of being are the right way and their spouses are wrong if they don't agree?

... AND THE TRUTH ABOUT MARRIAGE WILL SET YOU FREE

When God knit you together in your mother's womb (Ps. 139:13), He sculpted all your unique ways of being. Obviously, God doesn't give everyone the exact same package of personality traits, talents,

passions, dreams, preferences, bents, interests, tastes, likes, or wants
(even identical twins are different in some ways). With God, it is vive
la différence in how He makes each of us, and we are to respect that
uniqueness as we interact with our spouses.

I'm embarrassed to say I didn't think that way toward Holly
in the early years of our marriage. I think more that way now, but
I'm still working on it. God made Holly to be a sociable, happy-
go-lucky, sanguine person who always smiles; God made me to be
sensitive, introverted, and melancholic, and my face usually has a
serious look on it. God made Holly to be so carefree that when she's
walking, she trips a lot; God made me to be so cautious when I
walk that I look fifty feet down the road to avoid a face-plant. God
made Holly with such limited spacial (not "special," *spacial*) reasoning that she leaves enough room in a dishwasher to park a small
car after she loads it; God made me with such hypervigilant spacial
reasoning that you can hardly fit a toothpick in a dishwasher after
I load it. God made Holly gracious and compassionate; God made
me a prophet who tells you how you're messing up and challenges
you to get your act together. God made Holly heat sensitive such
that she wants the thermostat on sixty-eight degrees in the summer;
God made me cold sensitive such that I want it on seventy-eight
degrees in the summer. When it comes right down to it, Holly and
I are as different as night and day. But with God's help, we have
gone from a marriage in which we frequently fought over how different we are to a marriage in which we respect and support these
differences.

If you and your spouse fight over how different you are, understand that God wants to use your marriage to help you learn four

important things: (1) how to respect each other's differences, (2) how to support each other while remaining true to the unique way God created each of you, (3) how to get over the narcissism of thinking *you* are the measuring stick for how your spouse ought to be, and (4) how to compromise on your preferences but never compromise your convictions.

For example, never compromise on whether it is okay to lie. Lying is always wrong (conviction). But you need to be willing to compromise on how high or low you set the thermostat at night (preference). Never compromise on whether it is okay to steal. Stealing is always wrong (conviction). But you need to be willing to compromise on the restaurants you choose (preference). Never compromise on whether it is okay to cheat (in any way). Cheating is always wrong (conviction). But you need to be willing to compromise on which movies you see (preference).

When you are willing to compromise on the preferences in marriage, you are not giving away the *truly* important things about yourself that God meant you to be (your unique wiring and convictions). You are simply acknowledging that there happens to be another human being in your marriage, and that when it comes to your preferences, "you can't always get what you want" (thank you, Rolling Stones).[4]

Brenda and Chuck weren't fighting over convictions; they were fighting over preferences. Their unwillingness to meet each other halfway on the preferences stuff was causing them to spiral down into feeling bitter and resentful toward each other. There's nothing wrong with Chuck wanting to leave his jogging shoes beside their bed, but there is something wrong if he isn't willing to put them in the closet if Brenda is bothered by smelling them. There's nothing wrong with Brenda wanting the thermostat to be set higher at night, but there is something wrong if she isn't sensitive to how hot Chuck feels at night. There's nothing wrong with Chuck not being a fan of Italian food, but there is something wrong if he won't ever eat Italian food with Brenda or if he does, he has a bad attitude about it. There's nothing wrong with Brenda wanting to see movies in which "everyone cries all the time" (as Chuck passive-aggressively put it), but there is something wrong if she is bothered that Chuck likes movies that show "things blowing up and cars crashing into each other" and won't go see that kind of movie with him.

I don't say all of this to put Chuck or Brenda down. I'm just suggesting that it is toxic to be unwilling to accept that your spouse is different from you, to be unwilling to make compromises in the areas in which you are different, or to compromise but do so with a bad attitude. God means for us to be different, to respect those differences in each other, and to accommodate each other as best we can so that "as far as it depends on [us, we] live at peace with everyone" (Rom. 12:18). The most important "everyone" to you is your spouse.

One of my favorite verses in the Bible is Galatians 5:1: "It is for freedom that Christ has set us free." I know this verse is referring to Christ coming to earth and freeing us from being enslaved to sin, from having to pay off the debt accrued by our sins, from having to earn right standing with God, and from spending eternity separated from God. But at the risk of misapplying this verse, I also like to think that Christ came to set us free to be the one-of-a-kind individuals we are supposed to be.

To have a healthy and intimate marriage, both people must remain true to whom *God* meant them to be, never give up on their convictions, and be open to properly compromising on their preferences. As spouses, we need to see that with God it truly is vive la différence in marriage. We need to understand that God never meant our spouses to be just like us, and that we are not supposed to react to our spouses' unique mixture of traits, qualities, and preferences by being critical, disapproving, or rejecting.

PUTTING TRUTH INTO ACTION: DO THE FAIR THING

Acknowledge (believing this lie): "I've bought into the belief that my spouse is supposed to think, feel, and act just like me and that my spouse is wrong for being different from me. Both of those ways of thinking are lies and cause tremendous damage to our marriage."

In your own words, acknowledge believing this lie:

_____

_____

_____

_____

_____

_____

_____

Assess (the cost of believing this lie): "Believing this lie has made me feel superior, pull away, and criticize my spouse. I have failed to get behind my spouse's unique traits that are like no one else's on the planet. All of this has led my spouse to feel unsafe with me, hide qualities that are not like my own, and be less than the complete person God designed my spouse to be."

In your own words, assess the marital cost of believing this lie:

_____

_____

_____

_____

_____

_____

Adopt (biblical truth):

"For you created my inmost being; you knit me together in my mother's womb. I praise you because I am fearfully and wonderfully made; your works are wonderful, I know that full well" (Ps. 139:13–14).

"We have different gifts, according to the grace given to each of us" (Rom. 12:6).

"If it is possible, as far as it depends on you, live at peace with everyone" (Rom. 12:18).

"Let us therefore make every effort to do what leads to peace and to mutual edification" (Rom. 14:19).

"For we are God's handiwork, created in Christ Jesus to do good works, which God prepared in advance for us to do" (Eph. 2:10).

Write down biblical truths that will help you defeat this lie:

_____

_____

_____

_____

_____

_____

Act (on truth): Write down the ways your spouse is different from you in terms of his or her God-wired traits, gifts, interests, talents, and qualities. Be on the lookout for these to show up, and affirm your spouse for being that way. On the flip side, refrain from criticizing the things your spouse is or does that are stylistically different from the things you are or do. Support your mate's uniqueness by doing things your mate likes to do, whether you like doing them or not.

In your own words, describe how you will put truth into action:

_____

_____

_____

_____

_____

_____

Ask (for forgiveness): "I want to apologize for being critical of how you are just because you're different from me. Please forgive me for being so arrogant that I would think my way of being me is superior to your way of being you. God has made you with so many wonderful qualities, traits, gifts, interests, and passions, and they are all woven together in a way that makes you special, truly one of a kind. I'm sorry I haven't supported you in being those things. I ask you to forgive me for that, and I hope you will pray for me as I try to support your efforts to be the person God wants you to be."

In your own words, ask your spouse to forgive you:

_____

_____

_____

_____

_____

_____

_____

PRAYER

God, we are all Your handiwork, we are all fearfully and wonderfully made, and we are all meant to be unique. Please help me accept that my spouse and I are different rather than be at odds with that fact. Help me look for opportunities to affirm my spouse's special qualities, abilities, and gifts. Please help me think highly of the ways You have made my spouse that are different from how You have made me. Help me, God, to not think more highly of myself than I ought, to realize the unique way You have made me doesn't mean I am better or more special than my spouse. Please help me support the way You have uniquely fashioned my spouse. In the precious name of Jesus Christ and by the power of the Holy Spirit. Amen.

CHAPTER 9

I CAN SEE CLEARLY NOW

Lie #8: I see my spouse for who my spouse really is

*The mind is its own place, and in itself can make
a heaven of hell, a hell of heaven.*
—John Milton, *Paradise Lost*

For now we see only a reflection as in a mirror.
—1 Corinthians 13:12

The Hubble telescope has sent back some incredible images since it first went into space in 1990. Some of the pictures of nebulae, solar systems, and galaxies will make your jaw drop. But did you know that the first images sent back were not nearly as sharp as what was hoped for? And did you know that scientists discovered, much to their dismay, that the people who made the lens had improperly ground the main mirror for the telescope? Lots of technical savvy and millions of dollars were poured into coming up with a solution to correct the problem. Eventually, images started pouring in that have left us awestruck.

I bring all of this up because a lot of us think we have an accurate image in our mental telescopes of our spouses. We might not say it out loud for public consumption, but we think we see our spouses for who they truly are. But the truth of the matter is that no husband or wife has an accurate view of his or her spouse. And after thousands of hours of listening to couples describe each other, I would say most of us have a *largely inaccurate* view of who our spouses really are.

This chapter will take you deeper into the lie "I see my spouse for who my spouse really is." I want to show you some of the ways you mentally distort who your spouse is, similar to what you see when you stand in front of one of those wavy mirrors at a circus or fair and you look like anyone but who you are. To have healthy marriages, we must acknowledge that we have highly distorted images of our spouses and that our inaccurate images have led us to react to our spouses in very hurtful and wounding ways. Let's get some input on just how blurred our vision is when it comes to our spouses.

THE LIE: I SEE YOU EXACTLY FOR WHO YOU ARE

Paul Simon believes there are "Fifty Ways to Leave Your Lover."[1] Well, I believe there are "Fifty Ways to *Distort* Your Lover." In this section, I'm going to explore seven ways we mentally distort who our spouses really are. I'm covering only seven because I don't want to depress anyone with just how distorted a view we actually have of our mates.

I want to give credit where credit is due and acknowledge that I'm borrowing these seven cognitive distortions from Aaron Beck's book *Love Is Never Enough*[2] and David Burns's book *Feeling Good Together*.[3] Beck and Burns, both psychiatrists, are pioneers in the field of cognitive therapy, an approach to helping people overcome mood problems, difficulties handling life stress, and conflict in relationships by changing faulty thinking (sound anything like the book you are reading?).

With no further ado, here are the Un-magnificent Seven Styles of Distorted Thinking in Marriage:

1. *Magnification.* This is the tendency to make a mountain out of a molehill, or to make more of something than it actually is (such as your spouse's negative qualities). For example, let's say your husband tends to watch too much television. You are magnifying this trait when you decide he is a couch potato. Here, magnification led you to see your husband as worse than he really is.

2. *Minimization.* This is the tendency to make a molehill out of a mountain, or to make less of something than it really is (such as your spouse's good qualities). Let's say your wife is a fairly disciplined person, but you think that she's just okay at personal discipline. Here, minimizing a positive quality in your wife led you to see her as worse than she really is. The same is true

when you minimize negative qualities. Let's say your husband has a really bad temper but you think that he just gets a little bit miffed at times. Now you are seeing your spouse as better than he really is.

3. *Personalization.* This occurs when you take on your spouse's behavior (usually his or her mistreatment of you), as if it is about you rather than your spouse. For example, let's say the two of you go to a dinner party and your spouse ignores you all evening. You are taking your spouse's behavior personally if you think you must not be worth paying attention to. What you should consider instead is that your spouse is being insensitive (or seeking other's approval, getting distracted, and so on), and it's not about you.

4. *Polarization.* This occurs when you take something about your spouse that is actually a shade of gray and you view in black-and-white, all-or-nothing, or never-or-always terms. For example, let's say your spouse *occasionally* arrives home late and you turn it into "You never come home on time!" Or your spouse at times spends too much money and you think he or she is a spendaholic.

5. *Overgeneralization.* This is the tendency to take a particular trait about your spouse and assume

he or she is always going to be that way. Let's say your spouse tends to job hop. You might overgeneralize by assuming he or she is never going to keep a job for very long. Here, you take something your spouse did and use it to predict your spouse is going to be that way in the future.

6. *Selective Abstraction.* This is the mental tendency to miss the forest for the trees. Here you mentally lock in on a particular trait about your spouse (usually a negative one) and lose sight of all the rest of your spouse's traits. For example, you focus solely on the fact that your spouse has poor table manners and ignore the fact that he or she is a good listener, genuinely cares about others, or reaches out to comfort people when they are hurting.

7. *Emotional Reasoning.* This involves believing your feelings reflect the ways things actually are. For example, you *feel* your spouse is a selfish jerk, so you conclude your spouse *is* a selfish jerk. Here, you make the assumption you can trust your feelings (because your feelings wouldn't lie to you) and you allow how you feel to determine your view of reality.

To help you identify how these distortions might come into play in your marriage, read the following interaction between Dan and

Cheryl, all the while looking for these seven cognitive distortions in how they see each other. Just to give you a little help, I've highlighted (by using italics) the words and phrases that should tip you off about which of the seven distortions Dan and Cheryl are falling into.

Dan: You *never* listen to me!

Cheryl: I do too. I listen to you *all the time.*

Dan: *No, you don't!* I asked you to get some coffee at the grocery store the other day, and you forgot!

Cheryl: You asked me to get a bunch of things at the grocery store, and *all you pay attention to is the one thing I forgot!* Really?

Dan: Well, that was *a pretty big thing to forget* … You know I have to have my cup of coffee every morning before I leave for work.

Cheryl: Aren't you making *too big a deal* out of this?

Dan: Well, *you didn't forget anything* at the store that *you wanted.*

Cheryl: Oh, so I forgot what you wanted because *I never think about you*, is that it?

Dan: How else am I supposed to take it when you get everything you want and *don't get what I want?*

Cheryl: Well, you might consider not taking it as a *personal affront.*

Dan: Well, *if you really cared about me*, you wouldn't have forgotten my coffee!

Cheryl: So, I forget your coffee, and all of a sudden *I don't care about you?* You've got to be kidding! The other day, I asked you to mail some letters for me, and they're still on your desk. Does that mean you never listen to me and don't care about me?

Dan: Oh, forget it. I don't want to talk about it anymore. *In the future*, just don't forget my coffee.

Cheryl: Well, *in the future*, don't forget to mail my letters!

Dan started things off badly when he accused Cheryl of "never" listening to him. What distorted style of thinking is that? That's right, *polarization*. At the same time, Dan was also *minimizing* Cheryl's listening skills, which were actually quite good. Cheryl fired back with her own version of *polarization* when she informed Dan she listens to him "all the time" (which, by the way, no one does).

Cheryl got back at Dan when she pointed out that the only thing he paid attention to was what she *didn't get* for him at the grocery store. What was she accusing Dan of doing? That's right, *selective abstraction*. Dan then made things worse when he said Cheryl's forgetting to buy his coffee was a "pretty big thing." What style of distorting reality is that? Right, *magnification*. Cheryl's moving to Montana to get away from Dan would have actually been a "pretty big thing," but forgetting Dan's coffee was not.

When Dan accused his wife of remembering everything *she* wanted at the store but not everything *he* asked for, he fell into *personalization*. Dan responded as if Cheryl's forgetting his coffee were a reflection of him somehow not being important enough to remember his request instead of Cheryl simply forgetting, getting distracted in the store, or (worst-case scenario) being too focused on what she wanted to get. In taking her actions personally, Dan wasn't able to see that Cheryl's forgetting his coffee was actually about Cheryl (that she doesn't have a perfect memory, gets distracted, or actually does hate his guts and wants to punish him for being such a lousy husband).

Dan fell into *emotional reasoning* when he told Cheryl, "If you really cared about me, you wouldn't have forgotten my coffee!" Here, Dan turned his feelings into a fact when he said Cheryl doesn't care about him because she forgot his precious coffee (sorry, I'm a little frustrated with Dan here).

Both put the cognitive distortion cherry on top of the cake by falling into *overgeneralizing* when they said, "In the future ..." Both fell into thinking that the past always predicts the future and that neither of them was going to be different down the road.

Now, if you asked Dan and Cheryl if they saw each other accurately, both of them would say yes. I know because I asked them that question during one of our counseling sessions. But now that you know about the ways the two of them distorted each other's behavior and imperfections, do you think Dan and Cheryl see each other accurately? No, not even close.

Keep in mind that all of these seven styles of distorted thinking come into play the moment you first meet your spouse to be, but just in a positive direction. When we fall in love, we tend to magnify each other's positive qualities ("She is the kindest person I have ever met"), minimize each other's negative traits ("It's no big deal that he spent time in prison for armed robbery"), personalize the fact that the other person worships the ground we walk on ("I must be pretty awesome given she thinks I'm so awesome"), polarize each other ("He's such an amazing person"), overgeneralize about how the person is going to be in the future ("She's always going to be so gracious and forgiving"), focus on one of his or her most wonderful qualities at the expense of seeing other qualities ("Isn't he the most incredible hunk of burning love you have ever laid your eyes on?"), and let our feelings dictate how we view reality ("I'm just so in love I can't see straight—she must be the one for me").

I don't mean to rain on anyone's parade here, but falling in love can be a form of delusional psychosis in that you are almost completely out of touch with the reality of who your future mate is as a human being. That is why I wanted each of my children to date the person he or she wanted to marry for *twenty-five years* before getting married (I'm kidding here, but only a little). I wanted my kids to fall in love and marry, but I didn't want them to delude themselves into thinking they actually saw their future spouses for who they really are.

The idea that "I see my spouse for who my spouse really is" is a lie because of the natural fallen bent *every human being* has toward mentally distorting reality. Dan and Cheryl didn't see each other accurately because they had a tendency to magnify each other's negative qualities, minimize each other's positive qualities, take each other's actions personally, view each other in black-and-white terms, believe the other person was never going to change, selectively pay attention to the things the other did wrong at the expense of seeing the things the other did right, and let their feelings dictate reality. Because they didn't see each other accurately, Dan and Cheryl weren't interacting with the real person but with a Frankenstein-like monster they had turned the other person into in their minds. You can't mentally turn your spouse into a monster and then hope to get along in a loving, caring way.

All of us distort what our spouses do and who our spouses are, and we do it to a pretty significant degree. Because we don't see our spouses for who they are, we don't treat them the way they are supposed to be treated. From the day we first fell in love with our spouses and saw them much too positively to the present day when most of us see our spouses much too negatively, we haven't seen our husbands and wives as they truly are.

"I can see [my spouse] clearly now." Not really.

So, what are husbands and wives to do if, by virtue of these seven ways of distorting reality, they have turned their spouses into versions of the Frankenstein monster?

... AND THE TRUTH ABOUT MARRIAGE WILL SET YOU FREE

Just as the Hubble telescope's view of space needed to be repaired, so our view of our spouses needs to be repaired as well. We all need to go in for corrective eye surgery if we are going to see our spouses for who they really are and treat them the way God wants us to.

What insight does the Bible offer about how to correct our distorted views? It gives us all kinds of principles for how to see people more accurately, but I want to touch on just one we need to get much better at implementing if we want to break free from faulty ways of viewing our mates: "Finally, brothers and sisters, whatever is true, whatever is noble, whatever is right, whatever is pure, whatever is lovely, whatever is admirable—if anything is excellent or praiseworthy—think about such things" (Phil. 4:8).

I want to apply this principle to marriage to help us better understand how we are supposed to think about our spouses. We are supposed to focus on thoughts that are true, noble, right, pure, lovely, and admirable. We are to view our spouses the way the *corrected* Hubble telescope now views planets, nebulae, solar systems, and galaxies—in all their grandeur, beauty, and awesomeness. Let's quickly go through the list of "whatever is … think about such things" to get a better sense of how to apply it to marriage.

- *Whatever is true:* We are supposed to see our spouses accurately, as they really are. We are to guard against seeing things that are not actually there, things that are false.
- *Whatever is noble:* We are supposed to focus on those things about our spouses that are admirable and honorable.
- *Whatever is right:* We are supposed to give our spouses credit where credit is due as far as how they are in conformity with who God wants them to be.
- *Whatever is pure:* We are to think about our spouses in a morally wholesome and sexually pure way. We are not to have unchaste thoughts about them.
- *Whatever is lovely:* We are to think about our spouses' pleasing, attractive, and agreeable traits, not camp out on their displeasing qualities.

- *Whatever is admirable:* We are to think about our spouses' positive, constructive, and mature qualities, those qualities that give them a good reputation with others.

As husbands and wives, we have this problem: our "mental mirrors" came with defects, and these defects cause us to have images of our spouses that are fuzzy, cloudy, and distorted. Just as the Hubble space telescope initially had improperly sculpted mirrors, causing it to send back images of celestial reality that were less than what was hoped for, we come into the world with improperly sculpted ways of viewing reality that cause us to have unclear and inaccurate images of our spouses.

Consequently, our humanness makes us incapable of seeing our spouses, others, ourselves, and God in a distortion-free way. That is why we can't allow our natural way of viewing to dictate our perceptions of who our spouses actually are. We desperately need *supernatural* help to see our spouses in ways that are "true ... noble ... right ... pure ... lovely ... admirable." We all need supernatural help in the form of the Holy Spirit, whose job it is to "guide [us] into all the truth" (John 16:13) when it comes to how we think about our mates.

Each day we need to ask the Holy Spirit to help us "take captive every thought to make it obedient to Christ" (2 Cor. 10:5) and help us think on what is "true ... noble ... right ... pure ... lovely ... admirable" in our marriages. We need Him to help us "be transformed by the renewing of [our minds]" (Rom. 12:2). We need Him to guide us away from thoughts that are untrue, ignoble, wrong, impure, unlovely, and unadmirable about our spouses and guide us toward thoughts that are in the opposite direction.

As always our role model is Christ. He never had a distorted view of people He interacted with. He never saw people as better or worse than they were; He saw them exactly as they were. Christ never took what people did as a personal affront; how a person treated Him was His clue about that person's spiritual condition. Christ was never black-and-white about people; He saw everything about a person in its appropriate shade of gray. Christ never predicted people's futures from their pasts; He let others know they could chart a better course anytime they wanted to. Christ never focused on a specific detail about a person at the expense of the big picture; He never lost sight of the fact that He was dealing with "fearfully and wonderfully made" (Ps. 139:14) image bearers, even if they were acting like hellions. And Christ never allowed His emotions to dictate how He viewed reality; He allowed Himself to have strong emotions, but His emotions never dictated what He believed the truth was or what choices He made. Christ saw every person *exactly* for who he or she was. And although Christ knew every person's imperfections and sometimes challenged that person on his or her less-than-favorable traits, He never once strayed from thinking on "whatever is true … noble … right … pure … lovely … admirable … excellent or praiseworthy" about someone. That, my friends, is a lot more impressive than turning water into wine.

Wouldn't you like to see your spouse for who he or she really is? Wouldn't you like, perhaps for the first time, to see your mate clearly, accurately, and in a distortion-free way? Ask God to help you correct the view you have of your spouse. As you begin to abandon your distorted views, you are likely to realize you have a whole different person on your hands—and you didn't even have to marry someone else for it to happen!

PUTTING TRUTH INTO ACTION: DO THE FAIR THING

Acknowledge (believing this lie): "I believed the lie that I see my spouse for who my spouse really is. But the truth of the matter is, I don't. I look at a reflection of my own making and have been interacting with a person of my own flawed creation. I have made my spouse's bad qualities worse and ignored my spouse's many wonderful qualities. I have taken my spouse's actions as a personal affront and responded hurtfully as a result. And I have arrogantly presumed that the past will dictate who my spouse will be in the future. By thinking these ways, I have treated my spouse in an unloving and ungracious manner and have not made the marriage a safe place. I have far to go in seeing my spouse as God does, and I desperately need His help to make the journey."

In your own words, acknowledge believing this lie:

_____

_____

_____

_____

_____

_____

Assess (the cost of believing this lie): "Because I don't see my spouse for who my spouse actually is, I have overreacted, withheld affirmation, become bitter and resentful, failed to encourage my spouse about becoming a better person over time, and made it impossible for us to discuss our different ways of viewing each other in a safe, respectful manner. All of this has made my interactions with my spouse toxic, wounding, and destructive."

In your own words, assess the marital cost of believing this lie:

_____

_____

_____

_____

_____

_____

_____

Adopt (biblical truth):

"Test me, LORD, and try me, examine my heart and my mind" (Ps. 26:2).

"You desired faithfulness even in the womb" (Ps. 51:6).

"Buy the truth and do not sell it" (Prov. 23:23).

"Let us walk in the light of the LORD" (Isa. 2:5).

"Love the Lord your God with all your heart and with all your soul and with all your mind" (Matt. 22:37).

"Be transformed by the renewing of your mind" (Rom. 12:2).

"Finally, brothers and sisters, whatever is true, whatever is noble, whatever is right, whatever is pure, whatever is lovely, what is admirable—if anything is excellent or praiseworthy—think about such things" (Phil. 4:8).

"Be alert and of sober mind" (1 Pet. 4:7).

"God is light; in him there is no darkness at all" (1 John 1:5).

Write down biblical truths that will help you defeat this lie:

_____

_____

_____

_____

_____

_____

_____

Act (on truth): Identify the style of distorted thinking you do the most toward your spouse, and write out an argument against thinking that way. If you tend to focus on a bad quality about your spouse at the expense of seeing good qualities, write down all your spouse's good qualities and share your list with your spouse. If you tend to frame your spouse's behavior in polarized terms ("You always interrupt me"), push yourself to come up with the "shade of gray" term that applies ("Sweetheart, sometimes you interrupt me when I'm talking") and express that truth to him or her. If you tend to minimize good qualities about your spouse ("Jill, you're kind of an honest person"), find the right words to describe how your spouse really is ("Jill, you're a very honest person") and express that.

In your own words, describe how you will put this truth into action:

_____

_____

_____

_____

_____

_____

_____

Ask (for forgiveness): "Sweetheart, I have such a distorted view of who you are. I tend to …" Finish this sentence by confessing the way you misperceive your spouse, for example, *make your bad qualities worse, make your good qualities less than what they are, take your actions personally, miss seeing the shade of gray about you, presume to judge how you are going to be in the future, not see the big picture of who you are, allow my feelings to determine how I view you.* Then continue by saying, "I am sorry I don't think on the things that are true, noble, right, pure, lovely, and admirable when it comes to you, and I hope you will forgive me. Please pray that I will grow to see you the way God sees you."

In your own words, ask your spouse to forgive you:

_____

_____

_____

_____

_____

_____

PRAYER

God, there are no flaws or distortions in how You view me or my spouse. You see us exactly for who we are, making us neither worse nor better. Because You see us for who we are, we can trust You when You hold up a mirror for us to look into about ourselves. Even though it is painful, I know You do that to help us grow into more mature and complete people. God, please help me see my spouse the way You do, rather than as better or worse than my spouse actually is. And if You lead me to hold up a mirror for my spouse to look into, please help me to hold up a mirror that has few, if any, flaws or distortions in it so that my spouse can feel loved, safe, and protected. In the precious name of Jesus Christ and by the power of the Holy Spirit. Amen.

CHAPTER 10

LET'S MAKE A DEAL

Lie #9: My spouse has to earn my forgiveness

He that cannot forgive others, breaks the bridge over
which he himself must pass if he would ever reach
heaven; for everyone has need to be forgiven.
—George Herbert

Bear with each other and forgive one another
if any of you has a grievance against someone.
Forgive as the Lord forgave you.
—Colossians 3:13

"When are you going to let me off the hook?" Glen asked, a look of desperation on his face.

"For what?" Elaine responded, knowing full well what he was talking about.

"For my business failing, for having to sell our house and move into an apartment."

"I told you that you should have never started that business! But did you listen to me? No! You went ahead and did exactly what you wanted to do, like always!"

"I thought it was the best thing to do."

"I understand that, but I kept trying to tell you I didn't feel good about it, and you totally ignored me! And now look where we are! We live in a tiny apartment, and most everything we own is in storage. We can barely make ends meet, we had to pull the kids out of private school, and we're all miserable! *Why didn't you listen to me?*"

"I did listen to you ... I just did what I thought was the right thing to do."

"Well, how's that working out for you? We're supposed to make decisions together, Glen, and you made this one totally by *yourself*! And *your* horrible decision has completely blown up in *our* faces."

"I get that. I'm sorry; I really am. I know I've hurt you and the kids, and I am doing everything I can to make things right. But when are you going to stop punishing me for what I did?"

"Punishing you? I'm not punishing you!"

"Yes you are! Every day either you give me the cold shoulder or you're just flat-out hostile."

"Well, ever since *your* business failed, my life has been a nightmare! Do you understand how embarrassed I am that we had to file for bankruptcy? Do you see how humiliated I was to have to tell our friends we had to move because *your* business failed? Do you realize how hard it has been for the kids to leave a school they loved and go to one they can't stand? We lost everything because of you! *What are you going to do to fix this?*"

"I told you—I'm doing everything I can to make things better! When are you going to forgive me?"

"I'll forgive you when you make everything right!"

As noticeably imperfect human beings, we all do things that are wounding to our spouses. The fact that we hurt each other brings us to a central issue in marriage—forgiveness. A number of years ago, Don Henley sang about the importance of forgiveness in his poignant song "The Heart of the Matter."[1] From my perspective, these are the most touching lyrics of the song:

> *I've been trying to get down*
> *To the heart of the matter ...*
> *But I think it's about forgiveness, forgiveness*
> *Even if, even if you don't love me anymore*

Whether or not we forgive our spouses when they disappoint or hurt us can make or break our marriages. Because of our fallen bent toward behaving in selfish and immature ways, we are inescapably going to do or say hurtful things to our spouses, inflicting painful arrows to their hearts. Wounding your spouse is not something that *might happen* in marriage; it is something that is *going to happen*. So the million-dollar question is, Are you going to forgive your spouse when he or she does hurtful things?

When it comes to Satan's efforts to "steal and kill and destroy" (John 10:10) you and your spouse, one of his biggest hopes is that both of you will withhold forgiveness in a self-destructive effort to punish each other. I say "self-destructive effort" because, as Joyce Meyer, author of *Beauty for Ashes*, so insightfully noted, "Harboring unforgiveness is like drinking poison and hoping your enemy will die!"[2] When you withhold forgiveness, you are destroying not only your marriage but also yourself.

I want to use this chapter to explore a lie most of us seem to believe about forgiveness, a lie that keeps husbands and wives from offering this precious gift to each other. When we believe this lie and withhold forgiveness from our spouses, it ties God's hands in being able to turn this sacred relationship into a healthy and loving place.

THE LIE: MY SPOUSE HAS TO EARN MY FORGIVENESS

I saw the movie *Unbroken*[3] last week, and I haven't been able to stop thinking about it since. The film, which is based on Laura Hillenbrand's book by the same name,[4] is about the life of Louis Zamperini, an officer in the Army Air Forces during World War II whose B-24 experienced mechanical difficulties while on a mission and crashed into the Pacific Ocean. The movie especially affected me because my dad, like Louis, was commissioned as a second lieutenant in the Army Air Forces, trained as a navigator-bombardier, sent into combat during World War II, and flew extremely dangerous missions where he witnessed men being killed in the service of their country. We owe a tremendous debt of gratitude to all the men and women who have served in the military and put their lives at risk. Movies like *Unbroken* powerfully drive home just how much courage and bravery these individuals demonstrate and how much suffering they endure.

Louis Zamperini was adrift in the ocean with two other men who survived the crash. They had very little food and water and had to fight off shark attacks. One of the men, Francis "Mac" McNamara, died after thirty-three days. Zamperini and the pilot of the B-24, Russell Allen "Phil" Phillips, made it to the Marshall Islands after forty-seven days and were captured by the Japanese. Both Zamperini and Phillips were in prisoner-of-war camps for more than two years and were, to put it politely, abused and mistreated.

Zamperini's main tormentor was a prison guard by the name of Mutsuhiro Watanabe (nicknamed "the Bird"), whose special interest in physically and emotionally abusing Zamperini possibly stemmed from Zamperini being a famous Olympic athlete before enlisting in the Army Air Forces. The scenes in *Unbroken* in which the Bird abuses Zamperini were very difficult for me to watch. No animal should ever be treated that way, much less a human being. To his credit, Zamperini endured the abuse inflicted on him and returned to the United States in August 1945 to a hero's welcome.

The film doesn't portray this part of his life, but after the war, Zamperini had a severe case of what we now call post-traumatic stress disorder. He had horrible nightmares about his POW experience and began to drink heavily. His wife, Cynthia, attended a Billy Graham crusade in Los Angeles and became a Christian. She and some of her friends encouraged Louis to attend a crusade. He did so and ended up committing his life to Christ. After making that decision, love replaced hate and Zamperini forgave his captors—and his nightmares stopped. He began a new career as a Christian inspirational speaker and spoke all over the country on the topic of forgiveness.

Zamperini returned to Japan after the war and met with some of the guards who had treated him so badly, some of whom were in the very prison he had been in. He offered them forgiveness for how they had treated him. Watanabe, the guard who had been so cruel to Zamperini, refused Zamperini's overture to meet with him. Still, God enabled Zamperini to forgive all his former captors and experience the spiritual and emotional freedom of having done so.

If I had been physically and emotionally abused as a prisoner of war, I don't know if I would have been spiritually and psychologically healthy enough to forgive the people who tormented me. I'm not sure I would have had the same forgiving spirit that Louis Zamperini had toward these men. Instead, I think I would have been tempted to pray that these men would rot in prison for the rest of their lives and that the Bird would have been executed!

How about you? How do you think you would have responded? Would you have been able to offer your tormentors grace and forgiveness after what they had done to you over such a long period, with absolutely no remorse? If you could, you are a much better person than I. Painfully, I appreciate this quote from C. S. Lewis:

> Everyone says forgiveness is a lovely idea, until they have something to forgive, as we had during the war. And then, to mention the subject at all is to be greeted with howls of anger. It is not that people

think this too high and difficult a virtue: it is that they think it hateful and contemptible. "That sort of talk makes them sick," they say. And half of you already want to ask me, "I wonder how you'd feel about forgiving the Gestapo if you were a Pole or a Jew?"[5]

Why am I talking about the life of Louis Zamperini in a book about marriage? First, I can tell you why I'm *not* doing it. I'm not doing this because I'm equating what Zamperini experienced in prisoner-of-war camps to what most of us experience in marriage. There is no comparison. I'm talking about Zamperini's experience to suggest that in marriage most of us experience *significantly less* mistreatment but withhold *significantly more* forgiveness. That's a negative characteristic of husbands and wives, don't you think? Let's go back to Glen and Elaine, the couple I began the chapter with, to drive that home.

Glen wounded Elaine by unilaterally deciding to go into a risky business venture. Even though his intentions were good, he ended up losing all their money and got them into significant debt. As a result of his business failing, the family had to move out of their house, sell a lot of what they owned and move the rest into storage, take their kids out of private school, move into a tiny apartment, and file for bankruptcy. Glen was genuinely sorry for what he did, but he ran into what I call Elaine's "buzz saw of bile," her continual criticism about how much damage his failure had caused. Glen hoped his wife would forgive him, but because she was bitter and resentful about what he did, she was not going to. She let Glen know in no uncertain terms that she wasn't going to forgive him until he made "everything right." Elaine wasn't going to forgive Glen until they got out of debt, lived in a nice home, had the kids back in private school, overcame bankruptcy, and restored their social standing.

As far as I know, Elaine has never forgiven Glen for what he did. Despite his best efforts, Glen has not been able get them out of debt, they still live in a cramped apartment, most of their belongings are still in storage, they can still barely make ends meet, their kids are still in public school, and everyone is still miserable. From the way things look, Elaine won't forgive Glen for a long time, if not "until death do [them] part."

I'm not picking on Elaine here (or women in general—men are just as prone to withhold forgiveness from their spouses as women are), but I don't think Glen intentionally and maliciously inflicted these difficult consequences on his wife and family. But, even if he had, would it have been something that Elaine *couldn't* forgive? No, forgiving Glen wasn't a matter of *couldn't* for Elaine; it was a matter of *wouldn't*. Her heart was so encrusted with bitterness and resentment about the "sins" Glen committed that she was going to remain his unforgiving judge, jury, and executioner until he fixed everything.

Few things are more toxic to a marriage than unforgiveness. When spouses are unwilling to forgive, their resentment and bitterness poison the marriage and make it a deadly and unsafe relationship. Yes, we're back to the heart of the matter again. Forgiveness alone can heal a wound and allow a couple to reconcile. Unforgiveness truly is like drinking poison and hoping the other person dies.

I'm sure you didn't need me to use the last few pages to convince you that unforgiveness toward your spouse is wrong. Nor did you need me to convince you that some of us struggle to forgive our spouses for things that pale in comparison with how badly certain people have been treated throughout human history. But if you are like me, you need a reminder on occasion. And I'd like to remind us about what God has to say about forgiveness.

... AND THE TRUTH ABOUT MARRIAGE WILL SET YOU FREE

I want to walk you through what I believe to be the most important things the Bible says about forgiveness and to encourage you to incorporate these principles and concepts into your marriage. I've adapted this list from material found in Lewis Smedes's *The Art of Forgiving*[6] and R. T. Kendall's *Total Forgiveness*.[7] If you struggle with forgiving people who have hurt you, these two books are invaluable in helping guide you to a place of deep and genuine forgiveness.

Below is my list of the top-ten things the Bible has to say about forgiveness. Please read each point carefully, and let God help you believe it in the deepest part of your being so that you can forgive your spouse and heal your marriage. Follow the words of Psalm 51:6: "You desire truth in the inward parts, and in the hidden part You will make me to know wisdom" (NKJV).

1. Forgiveness is at the heart of Christianity. Christ came so that "everyone who believes in him receives forgiveness of sins" (Acts 10:43). As C. S. Lewis put it in *The Weight of Glory*, "To be Christian means to forgive the inexcusable, because God has forgiven the inexcusable in you."[8] If you don't understand the importance of forgiveness, you don't understand Christianity.

2. God commands us to forgive others. Ephesians 4:32 says, "Be kind and compassionate to one another, forgiving each other, just as in Christ God forgave you." God tells us to forgive our spouses when they hurt us. He is not asking, "Would you, please?"

3. Your spouse should not have to meet any requirements before you forgive him or her. As theologian Paul Tillich so succinctly stated in *The New Being,* "There is no condition for forgiveness."[9] You are to forgive whether or not your spouse acknowledges having hurt you, has stopped hurting you, or has made amends for hurting you.

4. If you withhold forgiveness, you don't understand how much God has forgiven you. In the parable of the unforgiving servant, a man owed his master an unpayable debt and was completely forgiven that debt (Matt. 18:21–35). Someone else owed this same servant the equivalent of a few dollars, and the servant had him thrown into prison for not paying him back. The unforgiving servant didn't grasp the size of the debt he had been forgiven. If he had, he would have never thrown a person into prison who owed him so little.

5. While God commands you to forgive your spouse, it is appropriate to ask that amends be made. The Bible talks a lot about people making things right when they do wrong things. If your spouse sins against you in "marital felony" ways or even in "marital misdemeanor" ways, he or she needs to do whatever it takes to make amends. For example, if your husband looks at porn on his computer, he needs to get a porn blocker that emails you whenever he tries to look at anything that has the slightest whiff of impurity. If your wife borrows your computer and breaks it, she needs to get it repaired. People aren't truly sorry for what they have done if they don't stop the wrong behavior and if they don't make amends.

6. *Forgiveness doesn't mean you forget what your spouse did.* When God said, "For I will forgive their wickedness and will remember their sins no more" (Heb. 8:12), I don't think He was saying He ever forgets the sins we commit. I don't believe God can forget the sins we commit against Him. I also don't believe we can forget the sins committed against us by other people. I think God is saying He chooses not to remember our sins. In marriage, we need to do the same for our spouses.

7. *Forgiveness doesn't mean you're saying that what your spouse did was no big deal.* Forgiveness, by its very nature, is about things that are a big deal (unfaithfulness, neglect, abuse, abandonment). Small offenses (being late, borrowing your stuff without asking, eating the snack you hid in the refrigerator) are not called "sins" in the Bible and probably don't warrant forgiveness. At the same time, if a spouse *repeatedly* commits a small offense (for example, chronically borrows your stuff without asking or comes home late from work and keeps you waiting), I believe that makes the behavior a bigger deal that needs to be forgiven.

8. *Forgiveness means you no longer hold what your spouse did against him or her.* When you forgive your spouse, you erase the debt accrued by the wrong behavior. When you forgive your spouse, you wipe the slate clean and view your spouse as not owing you anything. Psalm 103:12 says, "As far as the east is from the west, so far has he removed our transgressions from us."

9. Forgiveness is just as much for you as it is for the one who has hurt you. Lewis Smedes, in *The Art of Forgiving*, wrote, "When we forgive, we set a prisoner free and discover that the prisoner we set free is us."[10] You are doing yourself a huge favor when you forgive your spouse because you have just freed yourself from carrying around a five-thousand-pound weight of unforgiveness with you for the rest of your life. Not only does forgiveness benefit the person you forgive, but it also benefits you.

10. Forgiving your spouse does not mean you are reconciled or you are to attempt reconciliation. In the prodigal son parable (Luke 15:11–32), the father forgave his wayward son *before* his son had repented of his sinful ways. For the two of them to reconcile, however, the younger son had to repent of his "wild living." The father could *not* throw a welcome-home party until his son had repented of his wrongdoing. And it is important to notice that the father never once went into to the "distant country" where his son was squandering his wealth to attempt reconciliation. True reconciliation depends on the *offended* person being willing to forgive and the *offending* person being willing to stop sinning. As Lewis Smedes so rightly put it, "It takes one person to forgive. It takes two people to be reunited."[11]

Forgiveness is the heart of the matter in Christianity. The vertical dimension of forgiveness is such that when we put our faith in Christ, God forgives our sins. The debt accrued by our sins was marked "paid in full," and we are no longer at odds with our Maker. The horizontal dimension of this is that because our debt with God has been completely forgiven, we also need to "have forgiven our debtors" (Matt. 6:12) so that we are no longer at odds with them.

Please, forgive your spouse for how he or she has sinned against you. It will truly be the most Christian thing you have ever done and will be deeply healing for both of you.

PUTTING TRUTH INTO ACTION: DO THE FAIR THING

Acknowledge (believing this lie): "I believed forgiveness had to be earned, and that is a horrible lie. I have deluded myself into thinking I am justified to withhold forgiveness until my spouse stops doing wrong and makes everything right between us. I have made forgiveness conditional in my marriage, and as a result, I have also made love conditional. All of this is wrong and is me not thinking biblically about forgiveness."

In your own words, acknowledge believing this lie:

_____

_____

_____

_____

_____

_____

Assess (the cost of believing this lie): "Because I have withheld forgiveness, I have treated my spouse in a mean-spirited and wounding manner. I have acted as though I am better than my spouse when I am not. In refusing to forgive, I have treated my spouse coldly and caustically in our day-to-day interactions. I have refused to embrace my spouse's desire to make things right."

In your own words, assess the marital cost of believing this lie:

_____

_____

_____

_____

_____

_____

_____

Adopt (biblical truth):

"Forgive us our debts, as we also have forgiven our debtors" (Matt. 6:12).

"For if you forgive other people when they sin against you, your heavenly Father will also forgive you" (Matt. 6:14).

"Therefore, as God's chosen people, holy and dearly loved, clothe yourselves with compassion, kindness, humility, gentleness and patience. Bear with each other and forgive one another if any of you has a grievance against someone. Forgive as the Lord forgave you" (Col. 3:12–13).

"For I will forgive their wickedness and will remember their sins no more" (Heb. 8:12).

Write down biblical truths that will help you defeat this lie:

_____

_____

_____

_____

_____

_____

_____

Act (on truth): Write down the wrongs your spouse has committed that were the most hurtful to you. Go item by item, and ask God to help you wipe the slate clean. As each day passes by and these wrongs come to mind, ask God to help you continue to forgive as an ongoing process. When these past wrongs enter your mind, remind yourself, "I have already forgiven that particular wrong and am no longer holding it against my spouse. My spouse owes me nothing for committing that wrong, and today is a fresh start in our relationship."

In your own words, describe how you will put this truth into action:

_____

_____

_____

_____

_____

_____

_____

Ask (for forgiveness): "I apologize for having been unforgiving toward you. It was wrong of me to think of myself as superior to you. In withholding forgiveness, I have been committing the more grievous offense. To put conditions on forgiving you grieves God and is understandably hurtful to you. I am sorry for having been this way. Please forgive me, and pray that I will never let the sun go down on unforgiveness toward you in the future."

In your own words, ask your spouse to forgive you:

_____

_____

_____

_____

_____

_____

PRAYER

God, thank You for forgiving me of all the many wrongs I have done, wrongs that You feel deeply grieved about. Help me forgive my spouse as You have forgiven me, with no conditions or strings attached. Humble me, God, and help me see myself as no better or worse than my spouse. Help me remember You sent Your Son to die for the sins I have committed. Thank You for no longer holding those sins against me. Help me be that way toward my spouse, and help me come alongside my spouse in any way I can to help make things right between us. In the precious name of Jesus Christ and by the power of the Holy Spirit. Amen.

CHAPTER 11

STOP IN THE NAME OF LOVE

Lie #10: We can reconcile without repenting

Break up to make up, that's all we do
First you love me, then you hate me
That's a game for fools
—The Stylistics, "Break Up to Make Up"

Godly sorrow brings repentance that leads to salvation and
leaves no regret, but worldly sorrow brings death.
—2 Corinthians 7:10

"Sorry I'm late. I got hung up in traffic on the way here," Rich said as he hurried to the table where Kathleen was waiting.

"You're not going to blame the traffic for why you're late again, are you?" Kathleen snapped.

"Yes, as a matter of fact, I *am* going to blame the traffic for why I'm late. It was backed up because of a wreck. That's why I wasn't here sooner."

"So, let me get this straight. Are you saying you didn't wait until the last minute to leave work like you've done a million times before?"

"Why are you making such a big deal out of this?"

"I'm not *making* a big deal out of this! It *is* a big deal! You're late for everything we do. And it doesn't seem to matter how many times I tell you that it really bothers me. And by the way, I'm always on time—I never leave you waiting at a restaurant all by yourself."

"Boy, somebody woke up on the wrong side of the bed today."

"Don't patronize me. This isn't about *me*; it's about *you*. I've told you a thousand times ... *it really makes me mad when you show up late for everything*! And yet you keep doing it. That's why I know you're not the least bit sorry."

"Look, I told you I was sorry. What more do you want from me? Can't we just sit here and enjoy a meal?"

"*Saying* you're sorry doesn't mean you're really sorry. I want you to quit *saying* you're sorry and *show me* you're sorry by being on time."

"I can't promise I'll be able to do that ... "

"Well, then, I hope you enjoy eating this meal by yourself ... Maybe you'll finally get a taste of what it's been like for me all these years," Kathleen said as she stormed out of the restaurant.

Elton John had a hit song in the mid-1970s entitled "Sorry Seems to Be the Hardest Word."[1] I'm sorry, but I'm going to have to disagree with him on that. In a lot of marriages, *sorry* isn't the hardest word to say; it's the hardest word to say and really mean.

Sure, there are marriages in which *sorry* actually is the hardest word to say. In those marriages you can't pry the word *sorry* out of either spouse's mouth with a crowbar. But in the marriages described in this chapter, *sorry* isn't the hardest word to say; it's the easiest. In fact, *sorry* is said so easily and often that the word has lost any meaning. When said easily and often, the word is being used as a smoke screen to cover up that the person isn't genuinely remorseful about the wrong done. Here, *sorry* doesn't mean "I deeply regret that I've hurt you and won't do it again"; it means "I want you to see me as someone who cares that I've hurt you, sweep what I've done under the carpet, and enjoy my company despite what I've done."

A deadly lie is operating in a lot of marriages in which couples say the word *sorry* frequently but rarely mean it. This lie leads a lot of couples to think that they have reconciled (repaired the rupture in the relationship and have safely and intimately reconnected) with each other when they haven't, and that they can get along with each other when they can't. It leads to situations like Rich and Kathleen's, in which you either remain at a restaurant table grinding your teeth toward your spouse about his or her continued lateness or get up from the table and leave your spouse sitting there all alone.

THE LIE: WE CAN "CONTINUE TO SIN" AND STILL GET ALONG NICELY WITH EACH OTHER

In his book *The Prodigal God*, Timothy Keller suggests that the parable of the lost son "might be better called the Two Lost Sons."[2] I think he's right. Both sons were lost, just in different ways. The younger son was lost in that he was self-indulgent. He squandered his inheritance on wine, women, and song, with little if any remorse about how his behavior hurt his father and his older brother. The older son was lost in that he was self-righteous. He obeyed all the rules, dutifully worked the fields, and never squandered any of the things he had been given. As a result of each son's particular form of lostness, neither son had a loving, intimate relationship with their father or each other.

I don't think it is too much of a stretch to say that the younger son was the one who ultimately proved to be genuinely sorry for the wrongs he committed. How can we know? He did three things that showed he was sorry for just how deeply he had wounded his father: (1) he took ownership of his actions and admitted he had sinned: "Father, I have sinned against heaven and against you"; (2) he no longer felt entitled to being a member of the family and the privileges that went with it: "I am no longer worthy to be called your son"; and (3) he offered himself to his father as a servant: "Make me like one of your hired servants" (Luke 15:18–19). Those three things are the markers of genuine sorrow.

Now, compare the older son with the younger son. Did the older son admit to having sinned against his family by being self-righteous? No. Instead, he jumped on his father's and brother's cases about the sins he felt they had committed: "All these years I've been slaving for you and never disobeyed your orders. Yet you never gave me even a young goat so I could celebrate with my friends. But when this son of yours who has squandered your property with prostitutes comes home, you kill the fattened calf for him!" (Luke 15:29–30). Did the older son feel entitled to being a member of the family and having all the privileges that went with it, even though he was a self-righteous twerp? Yes. After working the field "all these years," he, as a member of the family with "all the rights and privileges thereto appertaining," had never even been given a goat, a goat he felt he richly deserved. Did the older son offer to help with the "your brother was lost and now is found" party the father was throwing? No. The older son resented that a party was even being thrown for his prostitute-chasing brother. He "became angry and refused to" join in the festivities (Luke 15:28).

Take a second to notice where each son ended up in the story. The repentant younger son accepted his father's forgiveness, was showered with gifts, and enjoyed a wonderful banquet with family and friends inside the tent. The resentful older son rejected his father's request to join the celebration, did not receive any gifts, and stayed all by himself outside the tent. The younger son's genuine sorrow led to joyful celebration. The older son's grandiose self-righteousness led to solitary confinement.

I believe the parable of the lost sons is the most important parable Christ told. In telling it, I believe He was trying to make some incredibly vital points about our relationship with God and about our relationships with each other. I think Christ was saying the following:

- We are lost when we live a life of license *or* legalism.
- Neither kind of life allows for a close, intimate relationship with God, or with any other human being.

- We should not wait until a lost person has stopped being lost to forgive him or her. (In the parable, the father ran out to greet his younger son, then sought out his older son and pleaded with him to join the party.)
- We can't genuinely reconcile with God or others if we continue to be self-indulgent or self-righteous.

Let's go back to Rich and Kathleen. I think Rich is the "younger son" in their marriage because he continued to take license arriving late when he and Kathleen were supposed to get together. But Rich is not a true younger son because he continued to run late all the time. He kept on sinning "so that grace may increase" (Rom. 6:1). Rich wasn't really sorry that his chronic lateness was hurting his wife. Consequently, he never sought her forgiveness or made amends.

I think Kathleen was the "older son" in their marriage because she was judgmental about Rich always being late (sorry, *frequently* being late), she thought being more punctual made her superior to Rich, and she refused to forgive him for his chronic lateness. Kathleen left Rich sitting at the table by himself, much as the older son wouldn't interact with his father or brother by refusing to join the party.

I believe both Rich and Kathleen were lost in their marriage, but in different ways. Neither felt genuine remorse about how wrong his or her actions were toward each other. Rich wasn't sorry he was frequently late, and Kathleen wasn't sorry she frequently looked down her nose at him. Both were unrepentant about their particular form of lostness, and neither stopped doing the things the other found wounding. Sadly, their marriage was going to keep paying the price in lost closeness.

Admittedly, I am talking here about spouses whose offenses include being habitually late and habitually superior. Compared with things such as lying, cheating, or stealing, being late or thinking you're better isn't as big a deal. Nevertheless, I'm using Rich and Kathleen's situation to drive home the idea that when a spouse isn't truly sorry for the wrong he or she does, regardless of the size of the wrongdoing, the rupture in the marriage cannot heal, and the couple cannot reconcile. It isn't the size of the wrong that damages a couple's chances of properly reconciling; it's the hardness of heart accompanying the wrong.

When husbands and wives express genuine sorrow by no longer doing the things that wound their spouses, their spouses can heal and the relationship can be restored to a deeply intimate connection. But when husbands and wives refuse to stop doing the hurtful behavior, they are dooming their marriages to be places of mistrust, hurt, and disconnection.

Please, in the name of love, stop doing the wrong things you do that hurt your spouse. Please stop giving yourself permission to arrive late, and stop giving yourself permission to feel superior if you are always on time. Genuine reconciliation cannot take place between you and your spouse if either of you keeps on sinning "so that grace may increase."

... AND THE TRUTH ABOUT MARRIAGE WILL SET YOU FREE

As I mentioned in the previous chapter, God commands us to forgive our spouses when they do something wrong. It doesn't matter how "big" the wrong was, it doesn't matter if your spouse has stopped doing the wrong, and it doesn't matter if your spouse is sorry for what he or she has done. When God commands us to forgive those who have wronged us, we need to obey Him and not look for an escape hatch.

The biblical truth I want to explore here, a truth that flies in the face of the lie that we can continue to do hurtful things but get along with our spouses and be reconciled with them, is this: "Godly sorrow brings repentance that leads to salvation and leaves no regret, but worldly sorrow brings death" (2 Cor. 7:10). Drawing from the parable of the lost son, let's explore what true sorrow looks like in a marriage. As we go through these biblical standards, consider whether you are practicing them in your marriage.

1. True sorrow requires that you take ownership and confess your sin to your spouse. When the younger son returned home, he confessed that he had sinned against his father (Luke 15:21). He didn't say, "Hey, Dad, good to see you! I'm starving; let's eat!" When you confess your sins to your spouse, you need to be specific about what you have done wrong ("I bought an eight-hundred-dollar handbag yesterday" or "I watched a sexually explicit movie last night after you went to bed"). Statements such as "I think I did something wrong, but I'm not sure what it was" or "I know you think I did something wrong, so you're going to have to tell me what it is" are not true confessions.

2. True sorrow requires that you feel the pain your spouse is in because of what you have done. This is called having empathy. Most of the time when our spouses are feeling hurt, we think about how bad *we feel* about what we've done, not about how bad our spouses feel about it. The younger son said to his father, "Father, I have sinned against heaven and against you" (Luke 15:18), and while I may be stretching things here, I think this statement suggests that the son had begun to have empathy toward his father for how his sins had been so hurtful to him. If you haven't empathized with how your spouse is hurting over what you did, you haven't reached a place of true sorrow yet.

3. True sorrow requires that you make amends. Saying "I'm sorry for what I did" but not doing anything to repair the rupture between you and your spouse is false sorrow that brings death to your marriage. The younger son planned to say to his father, "I am no longer worthy to be called your son; make me like one of your hired servants," but the father didn't let him finish his apology (Luke 15:19–24). Again, I can't know for sure, but I think this was how the son was going to try to make amends with his father—by serving in his father's house like the hired hands.

Genuine sorrow requires that you restore things to their original condition as much as you possibly can. For example, if you have unrepentantly been putting work ahead of your spouse, you make amends by spending less time at work and more time with your spouse. If you have not been taking care of things you are supposed to take care of, you need to make sure you do what you are supposed to do.

4. True sorrow requires that you are motivated to change your behavior because you want to help your spouse heal. Sometimes we are motivated to start acting better toward our spouses because we want to stop feeling bad about all the wrong things we have done. However, this kind of sorrow is *selfish* sorrow—we are motivated to change because we want to feel better and have our spouses take us back. True sorrow is *selfless* sorrow—we are motivated to change because we want to help the person we have wounded to heal.

I don't believe the younger son's only motivation for returning home was that he was hungry, though Scripture clearly says he was famished: "How many of my father's hired servants have food to spare, and here I am starving to death!" (Luke 15:17). I think two other reasons also motivated him: (1) he wanted to help his father heal from the pain he was in over his son asking for his inheritance early (which basically meant that the younger son wished his father were dead), and (2) he wanted to help restore his father's estate to its previous level of abundance by working as a hired hand. I may be giving the younger son more credit than he deserves, but I wonder if his return home wasn't largely motivated by his concern for how his father was doing and not by the fact that he was starving.

5. *True sorrow requires that you stop doing the wrong behavior.* Granted, when it comes to the wrong things we habitually do, we usually can't stop overnight. So the issue here is, Is your behavior trending in the right direction? If you are moving in the direction of doing wrong less and less and doing right more and more, you are demonstrating that you are genuinely repentant and truly sorry about what you have done. The younger son "got up and went to his father" (Luke 15:20), turning his back on the wild life he had been living.

I believe there is an important exception to the "trending in the right direction" standard when talking about a spouse's wrong behavior. Extremely grievous sins such as adultery, abandonment, neglect, or abuse must stop, and they must stop immediately. For example, a spouse should not be allowed to trend his or her way to being less adulterous over time. Just as schools have a zero-tolerance policy about certain behaviors that students simply cannot do without getting expelled (such as physically assaulting a teacher), husbands and wives need to have a zero-tolerance policy about certain types of sins. Spouses who do not immediately stop committing these kinds of sins should be asked to leave the home and must agree to marriage counseling if the marriage is going to continue.

I want to say one more thing about trending in the right direction. If, despite your best efforts to change, you find that like the apostle Paul, "I do not understand what I do. For what I want to do I do not do, but what I hate I do" (Rom. 7:15), you need to get more-serious help. Whatever you need to do to break out of bondage to a particular sin, do it. Get into a Christ-centered twelve-step program, an accountability group that will lovingly hold your feet to the fire about you changing your ways, an in-patient treatment program, or intensive, long-term counseling that is theologically solid. Don't let Satan keep you in "Egypt" by remaining enslaved to a particular sin. Get yourself into a theologically therapeutic version of "the wilderness" so that you can arrive in the land of "milk and honey."

In summary, if you want a healthy and thriving marriage, you and your spouse must own and confess the ways you have wounded each other. You must feel the pain the other is in, make amends, change so that your spouse will be better off, and be on a positive trajectory so that wrong actions decrease over time and right actions increase over time.

Please, for your own sake and for the sake of your marriage, stop telling your spouse you're sorry for the wrong things you do if you aren't willing to meet the five standards of true sorrow. Please stop hiding behind the words "I'm sorry," and start working on being genuinely sorry when you wound your spouse. Please stop your wrong actions in the name of love. You'll be doing yourself, your spouse, and your marriage the biggest favor.

PUTTING TRUTH INTO ACTION: DO THE FAIR THING

Acknowledge (believing this lie): "Even though I have often told my spouse I am sorry when I have done wrong, I have believed the lie that I don't have to change my behavior. I have believed the lie that we can still get along even though I continue to engage in sinful behaviors. It is wrong for me to think I don't need to change to be at peace with my spouse, and I desperately need God's help to have the kind of genuine sorrow that leads to becoming a more loving spouse over time."

In your own words, acknowledge believing this lie:

_____

_____

_____

_____

_____

_____

_____

Assess (the cost of believing this lie): "Because I have been unwilling to stop doing things that are hurtful, I have wounded my spouse and created an unsafe marriage in which my spouse doesn't feel protected. Rather than apologize for my actions and repent of them, I have defended what I've done and even made excuses. I have often turned the focus back on my spouse and the wrong things done to me. Because I have not repented of the wrong things I do, my spouse doesn't feel safe and secure in my arms and understandably has self-protectively pulled away from me."

In your own words, assess the marital cost of believing this lie:

_____

_____

_____

_____

_____

_____

Adopt (biblical truth):

"Turn from evil and do good; seek peace and pursue it" (Ps. 34:14).

"In the same way, I tell you, there is rejoicing in the presence of the angels of God over one sinner who repents" (Luke 15:10).

"I preached that they should repent and turn to God and demonstrate their repentance by their deeds" (Acts 26:20).

"Let us therefore make every effort to do what leads to peace and to mutual edification" (Rom. 14:19).

"Godly sorrow brings repentance that leads to salvation and leaves no regret, but worldly sorrow brings death" (2 Cor. 7:10).

Write down biblical truths that will help you defeat this lie:

_____

_____

_____

_____

_____

_____

_____

Act (on truth): Ask your spouse to give you a list of the things he or she has asked you to change but you have been unwilling to change. Go over that list together, and ask your spouse to pick one or two things and make a commitment to trend toward improvement in that area (or those areas). Agree to meet once a week with your spouse solely for the purpose of assessing how you are doing in your efforts to get better.

In your own words, describe how you will put this truth into action:

_____

_____

_____

_____

_____

_____

_____

_____

_____

Ask (for forgiveness): "I apologize for having been unwilling to make changes you have asked me to make. I apologize for saying 'I'm sorry' when I didn't mean it and for being defensive and making excuses for the wrong things I do. I apologize for turning the focus back on you when you are trying to express how you feel about my flaws. I apologize for expecting you to get along with me even when I continue to do things that hurt to you. I want you to know I am going to try to quit saying 'I'm sorry' if I don't mean it. Please pray that I not only would be open to your input about how I wound you but also would do something about it."

In your own words, ask your spouse to forgive you:

_____

_____

_____

_____

_____

_____

PRAYER

God, I know Your love is unconditional and Your forgiveness is complete, but I also know You are a righteous God who calls people to repentance. Help me experience true sorrow over my wrongdoing toward my spouse so that over time I become a more loving, gracious, and kind mate. Help me have more compassion and empathy about how my actions wound my spouse, help me put my sorrow into action by making amends, and help me do it for the betterment of my spouse. I have so much to change, God, and I desperately need Your grace and power to do it. Thank You for always being at work in me both to desire and to do Your good will. In the precious name of Jesus Christ and by the power of the Holy Spirit. Amen.

CHAPTER 12

JUST THE NEW OF US

Staying on the Path of Renewing Your Marriage

Just the two of us, we can make it if we try,
Just the two of us, just the two of us
Building castles in the sky,
Just the two of us, you and I
—Bill Withers, Ralph MacDonald, and William Salter, "Just the Two of Us"

Though one may be overpowered, two can defend themselves.
A cord of three strands is not quickly broken.
—Ecclesiastes 4:12

Our journey together through the lies we believe about marriage has come to an end. I want to commend you for having the courage to face the faulty beliefs you have about marriage. Not many people are willing to do that. I am confident your efforts will continue to bear much marital fruit for you and your spouse in the years to come.

I want to use this final chapter to suggest things you can do to maintain the gains you have made while working through this book. Specifically, I recommend you commit to these important fundamentals:

- Practice four particular spiritual disciplines together.
- Have three kinds of meetings with each other every week.
- Remind yourself each day who is on your side.

THE FOUR DISCIPLINES

You may have heard the statement "God can't steer a parked car." Well, I would say that God can't steer a parked marriage. God is committed to doing certain things on His end to help each of us have a loving marriage, but we have to do certain things on our end if we want the same. I believe practicing spiritual disciplines is a crucial part of what we need to do.

Let me walk you through four spiritual disciplines that, when done with your spouse, can help your marriage grow by leaps and bounds. If your spouse refuses to join you in practicing these disciplines, you can do them on your own and continue on the path toward personal growth and development. For a deeper exploration of all the spiritual disciplines, I encourage you to read Richard Foster's *Celebration of Discipline*.[1] In my opinion, it is one of the most important books about spiritual growth available and is an invaluable resource for how couples can strengthen their marriages.

1. Study

I tend to purchase things that require assembly and then fail to read the instruction manual when I put them together. I once did this when trying to assemble my daughter Kelly's new crib. It didn't go well. If I had read and followed the instructions, I would have had the crib done in about an hour. But because I didn't read the manual carefully, I ended up working on it all evening and into the wee hours of the morning.

If we want our marriages to be loving and healthy, we have to devote ourselves to studying "The Instruction Manual," the Bible. If we try to build a marriage without God's instruction, we risk messing up everything, resulting in a marriage that is not functioning as it was designed.

Psalm 119:15–16 says, "I meditate on your precepts and consider your ways. I delight in your decrees; I will not neglect your word."

Psalm 1:1–2 says, "Blessed is the one … whose delight is in the law of the LORD, and who meditates on his law day and night."

Second Timothy 3:16–17 says, "All Scripture is God-breathed and is useful for teaching, rebuking, correcting and training in righteousness, so that the servant of God may be thoroughly equipped for every good work."

The Bible is "a lamp for my feet, a light on my path" (Ps. 119:105), and we are being wise if we dedicate ourselves to studying what it has to say.

God has done His part by providing His Word and by indwelling us with the Holy Spirit, whose job it is to "guide … into all the truth" (John 16:13) and help us believe truth in our "inmost being" (Ps. 139:13). Our part is to study the Bible "like there's no tomorrow" so that we know not only what it says but also what it means.

If you want a loving marriage, study together.

2. Prayer

God uses prayer, one of the most important activities of a Christian's life, to change us. Christ had a solid, unwavering commitment to prayer: "Very early in the morning, while it was still dark, Jesus got up, left the house and went off to a solitary place, where he prayed" (Mark 1:35). In *Celebration of Discipline*, Richard Foster said, "In prayer, real prayer, we begin to think God's thoughts after him: to desire the things he desires, to love the things he loves, to will the things he wills."[2] Prayer gives God a crucial means by which to bring about a radical change both in who we are and, when it is His will, in the circumstances we face.

Many Christians use the ACTS method of prayer.

A stands for adoration, giving God praise for how great He is. Psalm 8:1 says, "LORD, our Lord, how majestic is your name in all the earth! You have set your glory in the heavens."

C stands for confession, or admitting your sins. First John 1:9 says, "If we confess our sins, he is faithful and just and will forgive us our sins and purify us from all unrighteousness."

T stands for thanksgiving, and involves expressing gratitude for all the ways God has blessed you, those you love, and the world at large. Ephesians 5:20 says that we should "always [give] thanks to God the Father for everything, in the name of our Lord Jesus Christ."

Finally, *S* stands for supplication, or asking God to meet your needs (things you need in order to live, like a job) and even your wants (things you desire but are not necessary to live, such as getting your dream job), and the needs and wants of others. Philippians 4:6 says, "Do not be anxious about anything, but in every situation, by prayer and petition, with thanksgiving, present your requests to God."

God has done His part by being ready, willing, and able to not only hear our prayers but also act on them according to His will for our lives. Even Christ, who is God, said to God the Father, "Yet not as I will, but as you will" (Matt. 26:39). We need to do our part and "pray continually" (1 Thess. 5:17).

If you want a loving marriage, pray together.

3. Service

To grow in your marriage, serve each other. The Bible says that Christ "did not come to be served, but to serve" (Mark 10:45). Even though He was God, Christ washed people's feet, gave them food, listened to them, healed them, had compassion toward them, and deeply cared for them. Interesting, isn't it, that when the disciples argued over who would sit at the right and left hands of Christ in heaven, Christ told them, "Whoever wants to become great among you must be your servant" (Matt. 20:26)? Greatness and servanthood are the same to God.

We all have a fallen bent toward wanting to be served, not serve. Among the interpretations of what "dying to self" means in the Bible, one certainly means dying to that selfish part of you that wants your spouse to serve you without you serving your spouse in return. Christ's life and teaching demonstrate that true greatness is in serving others.

Another version of serving I encourage you to consider as a couple is to serve a person, a group, or an organization outside your home. Hand in hand, volunteer at a soup kitchen, teach a Sunday school class, minister to the homeless, or go on a mission trip. Yes, we are to serve each other in marriage, but we are also supposed to serve hurting people in our community and around the world.

If you want a loving marriage, serve each other and serve the world.

4. Fellowship

God works through community. Speaking about the local church in the first century, the apostle Paul encouraged the early Christians about "not giving up meeting together, as some are in the habit of doing, but encouraging one another" (Heb. 10:25). Regarding marriage, we need the support that comes from being with other like-minded husbands and wives who are trying to have marriages that are pleasing to God. Unfortunately, a lot of us are choosing the Lone Ranger style of trying to improve our marriages, which sets us up for failure. English poet John Donne said, "No man is an island." Well, I would say, "No couple is an island." We must join with other couples to encourage, support, and challenge each other to have better marriages.

I think back over the years Holly and I have been married, and I am grateful for all the couples we have been with in small groups. These couples have been such a blessing to us as we all came together to work on being better spouses and better parents. You are too many to name, but you know who you are. Holly and I will never be able to thank you enough for all the ways you have been an encouragement to us. I want you to know that your fingerprints are all over this book.

If you want a loving marriage, fellowship with others.

Next, I'd like to walk you through three types of meetings I want you and your spouse to have each week. You can use these meetings to practice the four spiritual disciplines as you pray, study the Bible, serve by meeting each other's emotional needs, and enjoy each other's fellowship. Take these meetings seriously—they can be a way to meet the "minimum weekly nutritional requirements" of marriage and keep it healthy and vibrant.

THE THREE MEETINGS

There is an old hymn "Take Time to Be Holy"[3] by William Longstaff and George Stebbins that I loved when I was young. One of the phrases in the song that especially spoke to me as a child was "speak oft with thy Lord." For your relationship with God to grow, you have to take time to meet with Him and meet with Him often. Similarly, for your marriage to grow, you have to "speak oft with thy spouse." Here are three kinds of meetings that can help you do just that.

1. Staff Meeting

Once a week, for about thirty minutes, get together with your spouse and walk through your respective appointment books. Let each other know who is going to be where and when things are happening. This meeting is not for serious conversations about tension in your marriage. Stick to the facts during these meetings, and let your spouse know what *the next seven days* look like for you. If you have children, they will greatly appreciate the two of you doing this because it will mean that little Billy or Sally won't be left at basketball practice or swim lessons one day because Mommy and Daddy failed to clarify with each other who was supposed to pick him or her up.

2. Date Night (or Date Afternoon or Date Morning)

Once a week, for a few hours, go out and have fun by yourselves. Don't use this time to discuss your schedules or air your hurts. It's simply for enjoying each other's company and doing something fun. This may sound crazy, but I want you to purposely keep this time together shallow, superficial, light, and full of laughter. Do whatever you like to do, and in doing so, remind yourselves that you enjoy each other's company.

Don't be afraid of being silly during these dates. Give yourself permission to go do things that might make the two of you look foolish. If you go on a walk, lock arms and skip for part of the walk. If you want to do something new, go find an activity in town that might help you get over worrying about how things make you look to others (like those places where you're dropped into a vertical wind tunnel, or a dance studio where you can learn to square dance, or ...). I wish I had risked looking more foolish in life and had gotten over my need for others to see me as a mannered, refined, nonidiotic-looking human being.

3. Needs Meeting

Once a week, for an hour, spend time together focusing on the deeper things of your marriage. Here are the guidelines I want you to follow:

- Open with prayer.
- Share with each other how you are doing spiritually and psychologically *apart from the marriage.* Share your "inner world" so that your spouse can know you better in these areas of your life.
- Express a need (from the list of intimacy needs you created under "Act [on truth]" in chapter 3) that you would like your spouse to meet before your next meeting. Be clear about the specific need you want met and how you want your spouse to meet it. General statements such as "I want you to be more affectionate" don't help. Say something like, "I would like you to meet my need for affection by giving me a hug and a kiss before you leave for work, after you get home, and before we go to bed." And for goodness' sake, don't put your request in the form of a criticism like, "You really stink at being affectionate, so would you mind hugging me more often?"
- Read to each other from theologically sound books about having a healthy marriage or about

a topic of particular interest to you, and discuss
what you have read (see my recommended reading list at the back of this book).

- Close in prayer.

Agree on a specific day and time that each of these meetings will
take place. At the risk of sounding sexist, I recommend husbands
lead the way on this. Men, make sure the meetings are scheduled
and take place. Please do not put your wives in a position in which
they have to be the ones to schedule the meetings, go find you, and
remind you it's time to meet.

Don't take these meetings lightly. If the two of you will commit to
having these meetings no matter what, God will have an open door
to help you mature into an agape-loving couple.

NEVER FORGET: GOD IS ON YOUR SIDE

I pray that you "fight the good fight of the faith" (1 Tim. 6:12) in
developing the mind of Christ in your marriage. Stay mindful of the
lies you carry into your marriage each day and the powerful truths
that enable you to love your spouse in a rich and deep way. Staying
aware of both the faulty beliefs you have about marriage and the
correct beliefs you need to have is crucial in your efforts to have
the marriage you have always wanted. I encourage you to spend the
rest of your marital life thinking on "whatever is true ... noble ...
right ... pure ... lovely ... admirable ... excellent or praiseworthy"
(Phil. 4:8) about your spouse and not to allow the Enemy's efforts to
knock you off track get in your way.

As you seek to strengthen your marriage, don't forget that you have God on your side. Don't forget He is all-knowing, all-powerful, and everywhere at once and He's not the least bit intimidated by what you are up against in marriage (Rom. 8:31: "If God is for us, who can be against us?"). Don't forget He wants to "prosper you and not to harm you" (Jer. 29:11). Don't forget that as husband and wife, you are two strands, but that with God as the third strand, the two of you cannot easily be broken (Eccles. 4:12). And don't forget to collaborate with God in trying to improve your marriage as opposed to trying to do it on your own strength. Remember: "Unless the LORD builds the house, the builders labor in vain" (Ps. 127:1).

May God richly bless all that you do to honor Him with your marriage.

PRAYER

God, You are amazing. We cannot begin to grasp Your greatness. We acknowledge that Your thoughts are so much higher than ours and that Your ways are so much better than ours. We ask for Your continued help to guide us to truth, deeply believe truth, and put truth into action. Help us stop believing things that are false. Help us believe, in the depth of our being, the things that are true so that we might live lives that glorify You. God, please help us love each other the way You love us. Help us not to give in to the Enemy's efforts to destroy our union as husband and wife. Help us find joy in each other's arms, and help us cherish this time we have together. In the precious name of Jesus Christ and by the power of the Holy Spirit. Amen.

APPENDIX A

Biblical Teachings on Truth

Absence of Truth in the World

> So justice is driven back,
>   and righteousness stands at a distance;
> truth has stumbled in the streets,
>   honesty cannot enter.
> Truth is nowhere to be found,
>   and whoever shuns evil becomes a prey. (Isa.
>   59:14–15)

Therefore say to them, "This is the nation that has not obeyed the LORD its God or responded to correction. Truth has perished; it has vanished from their lips." (Jer. 7:28)

They exchanged the truth about God for a lie, and worshiped and served created things rather

than the Creator—who is forever praised. Amen.
(Rom. 1:25)

For the time will come when people will not put
up with sound doctrine. Instead, to suit their
own desires, they will gather around them a great
number of teachers to say what their itching ears
want to hear. They will turn their ears away from
the truth and turn aside to myths. (2 Tim. 4:3–4)

Christ's Claim to Be Truth

"Very truly I tell you ..." (John 5:19)

Jesus answered, "I am the way and the truth
and the life. No one comes to the Father except
through me." (John 14:6)

Jesus answered, "You say that I am a king. In fact,
the reason I was born and came into the world is
to testify to the truth." (John 18:37)

Consequences of Accepting Truth

Paul, a servant of God and an apostle of Jesus
Christ to further the faith of God's elect and their
knowledge of the truth that leads to godliness—
in the hope of eternal life, which God, who does

not lie, promised before the beginning of time. (Titus 1:1–2)

He chose to give us birth through the word of truth, that we might be a kind of firstfruits of all he created. (James 1:18)

Now that you have purified yourselves by obeying the truth so that you have sincere love for each other, love one another deeply, from the heart. (1 Pet. 1:22)

Consequences of Rejecting Truth

The wrath of God is being revealed from heaven against all the godlessness and wickedness of people, who suppress the truth by their wickedness, since what may be known about God is plain to them, because God has made it plain to them. (Rom. 1:18–19)

But for those who are self-seeking and who reject the truth and follow evil, there will be wrath and anger. (Rom. 2:8)

They perish because they refused to love the truth and so be saved. (2 Thess. 2:10)

Dedication to Truth

Show me your ways, LORD,
    teach me your paths.
Guide me in your truth and teach me,
    for you are God my Savior,
    and my hope is in you all day long.
        (Ps. 25:4–5)

Test me, LORD, and try me,
    examine my heart and my mind;
for I have always been mindful of your unfailing love
    and have lived in reliance on your
        faithfulness. (Ps. 26:2–3)

You desire truth in the inward parts. (Ps. 51:6 NKJV)

Teach me your way, LORD,
    that I may rely on your faithfulness;
give me an undivided heart,
    that I may fear your name. (Ps. 86:11)

I have hidden your word in my heart
    that I might not sin against you. (Ps. 119:11)

I have chosen the way of faithfulness;
    I have set my heart on your laws. (Ps. 119:30)

Buy the truth and do not sell it—
    wisdom, instruction and insight as well. (Prov. 23:23)

Do not merely listen to the word, and so deceive
yourselves. Do what it says. (James 1:22)

The Holy Spirit and Truth

When the Advocate comes, whom I will send to
you from the Father—the Spirit of truth who goes
out from the Father—he will testify about me.
(John 15:26)

When he comes, he will prove the world to be in
the wrong about sin and righteousness and judgment. (John 16:8)

But when he, the Spirit of truth, comes, he will
guide you into all the truth. (John 16:13)

Protection and Truth

Do not withhold your mercy from me, LORD;
    may your love and faithfulness always
        protect me. (Ps. 40:11)

Your word is a lamp for my feet,
    a light on my path. (Ps. 119:105)

Those who trust in themselves are fools,
  but those who walk in wisdom are kept safe.
    (Prov. 28:26)

APPENDIX B

Marital Lies versus Marital Truth

Lie #1: The purpose of marriage is to be happy

We tend to focus on being happy as we live out our lives, and this is no more evident than in marriage. A lot of us get married because we think doing so will make us happy, only to find out after we've walked down the aisle that marriage is hard work and leads to feeling unhappy at times. Couples who believe the purpose of marriage is to make them happy are in for a long, unhappy time together.

The purpose of marriage (apart from intimate companionship and raising godly children) is to help us mature into fully loving adults. *This* purpose of marriage is often associated with feeling unhappy because it requires that you die to self and sacrificially serve your spouse. Yes, of course God wants you and your spouse to experience happiness, passion, and excitement in each other's arms, but to get there, each of you, paradoxically, has to put your desire for happiness aside, focus on fostering your spouse's growth, and trust that happiness will come.

Lie #2: My spouse can completely meet all my needs

We tend to expect our spouses to meet all our relational needs, something that puts them under avoidable duress. No *one* person can meet all our needs, and no one should have to face that kind of pressure. Your spouse cannot be expected to provide all you need to get by in life. Human beings are finite, not infinite, and can give only so much.

Of course, God wants your spouse to meet a lot of your needs—the bar is set extremely high in marriage for how husbands and wives are supposed to satisfy each other's needs. But God has a wide variety of resources at His disposal for meeting the total package of your needs. Like it or not, God will not always work through your spouse to meet your needs.

Lie #3: My spouse is a bigger mess of a human being than I am

Some of us look down our noses at our spouses and think we are much better human beings than they are or will ever be. Granted, there probably are specific ways we are better than our spouses (more patient, more forgiving, and so on), but too many of us use that as a launching pad for thinking we are mostly better than our spouses. Consequently, we walk around with an air of superiority and treat our spouses condescendingly.

The truth of the matter is that if you compare yourself with Christ, you aren't significantly better (or worse) than your spouse. Christ is the measuring stick for how you are to assess yourself, and if you will compare how you live with how He lived His life, you won't ever look down your nose at your spouse again. We all "fall short of the glory of God" (Rom. 3:23), and not just a little. If you want to have a loving marriage, you must be humble and remember we are all fragile "jars of clay" (2 Cor. 4:7).

Lie #4: I am entitled to my spouse's love

We can all get a little full of ourselves in marriage. One of the main indicators of this is that we feel entitled to being loved by our spouses. Unfortunately, we enter marriage expecting to be loved, demanding to be loved, and feeling entitled to being loved. When we think we are entitled to our spouses' love, we end up unappreciative when our spouses are loving toward us and bitter and resentful when they aren't. Not being grateful when your spouse is loving and being bitter when he or she isn't are emotionally toxic places to be.

We are supposed to want or desire our spouses to love us; we are not supposed to feel entitled to their love. Given that God made you with needs, it is perfectly appropriate that you want your spouse to meet those needs. I would worry about you if you didn't want your spouse to meet them. But rather than demand that your spouse meet your needs ("You'd better meet my needs or else!"), humbly express this desire ("It would mean a lot to me if you would be willing to meet my needs").

Lie #5: Our marital problems are all my spouse's fault

The blame game is a real marriage killer. Anytime you blame your spouse for how the marriage is going, you are acting as if marriage is the tennis equivalent of playing singles rather than doubles. Sure, your spouse may be more to blame for a particular problem in the marriage, but that is not permission from God to blame him or her for *all* the problems going on between the two of you.

You will benefit from more humbly approaching your spouse with a "How are *we* going to fix the problems *we* have created in *our* marriage?" attitude, which is the only attitude you can afford to have if you want to play doubles successfully. The overall health or sickness of a marriage is a cocreated reality. Couples pool their collective strengths and weaknesses in marriage, and together, they create the state of the union.

Lie #6: My spouse should accept me just the way I am

We have a God-wired need to be accepted, "warts and all." Unfortunately, some of us think that because our spouses are supposed to accept us, it means we are off the hook for doing anything to remove our warts. But that is not what acceptance means. The idea that our spouses' acceptance of us means we don't need to change anything about who we are is seriously misguided and will lead us to hold on to things about ourselves that we need to let go of—things that hurt us individually and hurt our marriages.

You and your spouse have an "iron sharpening iron" responsibility to

- lovingly challenge each other to change the things about yourselves that are wrong and inappropriate;

- speak "the truth in love" (Eph. 4:15) to each
  other about the ways you treat each other
  badly;
- have firm boundaries about what is and is not
  acceptable in how you are being treated in marriage; and
- accept each other's shortcomings, but love each
  other enough to kindly and firmly challenge one
  another to be the people God meant you to be.

Lie #7: My spouse should be just like me

A lot of us translate being compatible with our spouses into "my
spouse needs to be exactly like me if we are going to get along."
Instead of respecting how different we are as individuals, we tend to
let these differences grate on us, sometimes to the point of driving
us crazy. Some of us don't actually want a spouse; we narcissistically
want a clone.

God makes every person unique, one of a kind. Our marriages
would bore us to death if our spouses were just like us. Hold on to
the special ways God meant you and your spouse to be when He knit
you "together in [your] mother's womb" (Ps. 139:13). Variety is the
spice of life, not something to be criticized, resented, or condemned.

Lie #8: I see my spouse for who my spouse really is

We sometimes give ourselves too much credit for seeing our spouses
accurately, for seeing them for who they really are. "I know you

like the back of my hand" is a patently false perspective to have in marriage because we always view the person we married through distorted eyewear.

To have a loving marriage, you must take off the lenses that cause you to have a skewed view of your spouse, and you must put on the lenses that correct your vision. Specifically, you need to stop making your spouse's flaws bigger than they are, making his or her strengths smaller than they are, being black-and-white about gray issues, taking your spouse's actions personally, focusing on a negative thing at the expense of seeing the whole forest of who your spouse is, predicting your spouse is always going to be the way he or she is, and allowing your feelings to dictate how you perceive your spouse and marital reality.

Lie #9: My spouse has to earn my forgiveness

Unfortunately, we tend to place conditions on forgiveness. We often set the bar so impossibly high for our spouses that no matter how high they jump, it will never be enough for us to forgive them. If your spouse has to meet certain conditions before you will forgive him or her, you are sentencing your spouse to a "works program" from which he or she can never be released.

God commands us to forgive others for the wrongs they do. We are not supposed to put any conditions on forgiveness. Forgiveness is independent of our spouses admitting to having wronged us, being sorry that they wronged us, and not wronging us anymore. Since God forgave you in the same way, it is the least you can do for your spouse.

Lie #10: We can reconcile without repenting

We are prone to excuse the hurtful things we do in marriage and to expect our spouses to "get along" with us anyway. It is the marital form of "wanting to do the crime but not wanting to pay the time." If you want to reconcile with your spouse after you have wronged him or her, you must first meet the standards of "godly sorrow."

To demonstrate godly sorrow, you must take ownership of what you have done wrong, feel the pain your spouse is in because of it, confess the wrong you have done, ask your spouse to forgive you, fix whatever you broke by making amends, and stop doing the wrong and hurtful things you have been doing. Anything less is not a genuine "I'm sorry," and you cannot enjoy a welcome-home party just yet.

RECOMMENDED READING

Aaron T. Beck, *Love Is Never Enough: How Couples Can Overcome Misunderstandings, Resolve Conflicts, and Solve Relationship Problems through Cognitive Therapy* (New York: Harper & Row, 1988).

Gary Chapman, *The 5 Love Languages: The Secret to Love That Lasts* (Chicago: Northfield, 2010).

Tim Clinton and Gary Sibcy, *Attachments: Why You Love, Feel, and Act the Way You Do* (Nashville: Thomas Nelson, 2009).

Henry Cloud and John Townsend, *Boundaries in Marriage: Understanding the Choices That Make or Break Loving Relationships* (Grand Rapids, MI: Zondervan, 2002).

Emerson Eggerichs, *Love & Respect: The Love She Most Desires, The Respect He Desperately Needs* (Nashville: Thomas Nelson, 2004).

Richard J. Foster, *Celebration of Discipline: The Path to Spiritual Growth*, 3rd. ed. (New York: HarperCollins, 1998).

John M. Gottman and Nan Silver, *The Seven Principles for Making Marriage Work: A Practical Guide from the Country's Foremost Relationship Expert* (New York: Crown, 1999).

Willard F. Harley Jr., *His Needs, Her Needs: Building an Affair-Proof Marriage* (Grand Rapids, MI: Revell, 2011).

Sue Johnson, *Hold Me Tight: Seven Conversations for a Lifetime of Love* (New York: Little, Brown and Company, 2008).

Timothy Keller and Kathy Keller, *The Meaning of Marriage: Facing the Complexities of Commitment with the Wisdom of God* (New York: Riverhead, 2013).

Kevin Leman, *Sheet Music: Uncovering the Secrets of Sexual Intimacy in Marriage* (Carol Stream, IL: Tyndale, 2003).

Mike Mason, *The Mystery of Marriage: Meditations on the Miracle* (Colorado Springs, CO: Multnomah, 2005).

Andrew Murray, *Humility: The Beauty of Holiness* (Old Tappan, NJ: Fleming H. Revell, 1997).

Les and Leslie Parrott, *The Good Fight: How Conflict Can Bring You Closer* (Brentwood, TN: Worthy, 2013).

Stan Tatkin, *Wired for Love: How Understanding Your Partner's Brain and Attachment Style Can Help You Defuse Conflict and Build a Secure Relationship* (Oakland, CA: New Harbinger, 2012).

Gary Thomas, *Sacred Marriage: What If God Designed Marriage to Make Us Holy More Than to Make Us Happy* (Grand Rapids, MI: Zondervan, 2002).

Leslie Vernick, *The Emotionally Destructive Marriage: How to Find Your Voice and Reclaim Your Hope* (Colorado Springs, CO: WaterBrook, 2013).

Milan Yerkovich and Kay Yerkovich, *How We Love: Discover Your Style, Enhance Your Marriage* (Colorado Springs, CO: WaterBrook, 2008).

NOTES

Chapter 1—Attitude Is Everything in Marriage

1. M. Scott Peck, ed., *Abounding Grace: An Anthology of Wisdom* (Kansas City, MO: Andrews McMeel, 2000), 19–20.

Chapter 2—And They Lived Happily Ever After

1. Fred Bronson, *The Billboard Book of Number One Hits*, 5th ed. (New York: Billboard Publications, 2003), 221.

2. "BMI Announces Top 100 Songs of the Century" BMI, December 13, 1999, www.bmi.com/news/entry/19991214_bmi_announces_top_100_songs _of_the_century.

3. "Happy Together," words and music by Garry Bonner and Alan Gordon, on *Happy Together*, recorded late 1966–April 1967 (Los Angeles: White Whale Records, 1967).

4. M. Scott Peck, *The Road Less Traveled: A New Psychology of Love, Traditional Values, and Spiritual Growth*, 25th anniversary ed. (New York: Touchstone, 2003), 81.

Chapter 3—You Complete Me

1. *What about Bob?*, directed by Frank Oz (Burbank, CA: Touchstone Pictures, 1991).

2. David and Teresa Ferguson, *Intimate Encounters: A Practical Guide to Discovering the Secrets of a Really Great Marriage* (Austin, TX: Intimacy Press, 1997).

3. *Jerry Maguire*, directed by Cameron Crowe (Culver City, CA: TriStar Pictures, 1996).

Chapter 4—The Plank in Your Eye

1. *The War of the Roses*, directed by Danny DeVito (Los Angeles: Twentieth Century Fox, 1989).

Chapter 6—It Takes Two to Tango

1. *Mr. and Mrs. Smith*, directed by Doug Liman (Los Angeles: Regency Enterprises, 2005).

2. *Mr. and Mrs. Smith*.

3. M. Scott Peck, *The Road Less Traveled: A New Psychology of Love, Traditional Values, and Spiritual Growth*, 25th anniversary ed. (New York: Touchstone, 2003), 35.

Chapter 7—I Yam Who I Yam

1. "I've Gotta Be Me," music and lyrics by Walter Marks (Burbank, CA: Reprise, 1968).

2. Carl Rogers, *On Becoming a Person: A Therapist's View of Psychotherapy* (New York: Houghton Mifflin, 1961), 283–84.

3. Frederick S. Perls, *Gestalt Therapy Verbatim* (Boulder, CO: Real People Press, 1969).

4. "Just the Way You Are," words and music by Billy Joel (New York: Columbia Records, 1977).

5. Aristotle, *The Nicomachean Ethics*, trans. Harris Rackham (Ware, Hertfordshire: Wordsworth, 1997), 27.

Chapter 8—Opposites ~~Attract~~ Annoy

1. Charles Lowery, *Comic Belief Volume 1* (Irving, TX: 6Acts Press, 2004), 39.

2. Adapted from the American Psychiatric Association, *DSM-IV and DSM-5 Criteria for the Personality Disorders*, www.psi.uba.ar/academica/carrerasdegrado /psicologia/sitios_catedras/practicas_profesionales/820_clinica_tr_personali- dad_psicosis/material/dsm.pdf.

3. "How Great Thou Art," words and music by Stuart K. Hine (Valencia, CA: Manna Music, 1953).

4. "You Can't Always Get What You Want," words and music by Mick Jagger and Keith Richards on *Let It Bleed* (London: London Records, 1969).

Chapter 9—I Can See Clearly Now

1. "Fifty Ways to Leave Your Lover," words and music by Paul Simon on *Still Crazy After All These Years* (New York: Columbia Records, 1975).

2. Aaron T. Beck, *Love Is Never Enough: How Couples Can Overcome Misunderstandings, Resolve Conflicts, and Solve Relationship Problems through Cognitive Therapy* (New York: Harper & Row, 1988).

3. David D. Burns, *Feeling Good Together: The Secret to Making Troubled Relationships Work* (New York: Broadway, 2008).

Chapter 10—Let's Make a Deal

1. "The Heart of the Matter," words and music by Don Henley, Mike Campbell, and J. D. Souther on *The End of the Innocence*, recorded 1988–89 (New York: Geffen Records, 1989).

2. Joyce Meyer, *Beauty for Ashes: Receiving Emotional Healing* (New York: Warner Books, 1994).

3. *Unbroken*, directed by Angelina Jolie (Burbank, CA: Legendary Pictures, 2014).

4. Laura Hillenbrand, *Unbroken: A WWII Story of Survival, Resilience, and Redemption* (New York: Random House, 2010).

5. C. S. Lewis, *Mere Christianity* (New York: HarperOne, 2009), 116.

6. Lewis B. Smedes, *The Art of Forgiving: When You Need to Forgive and Don't Know How* (New York: Ballantine, 1997).

7. R. T. Kendall, *Total Forgiveness: When Everything in You Wants to Hold a Grudge, Point a Finger, and Remember the Pain—God Wants You to Lay It All Aside* (Lake Mary, FL: Charisma House, 2007).

8. C. S. Lewis, *The Weight of Glory* (New York: HarperCollins, 1980), 182.

9. Paul Tillich, *The New Being* (Lincoln, NE: Bison, 2005), 9.

10. Smedes, *The Art of Forgiving*, 178.

11. Smedes, *The Art of Forgiving*, 27.

Chapter 11—Stop in the Name of Love

1. "Sorry Seems to Be the Hardest Word," words and music by Elton John and Bernie Taupin on *Blue Moves* (Universal City, CA: MCA Records, 1976).

2. Timothy Keller, *The Prodigal God: Recovering the Heart of the Christian Faith* (New York: Dutton, 2008), xvii.

Chapter 12—Just the New of Us

1. Richard Foster, *Celebration of Discipline: The Path to Spiritual Growth* (New York: HarperCollins, 1978).

2. Foster, *Celebration of Discipline*, 33.

3. "Take Time to Be Holy," words by William D. Longstaff, 1882, and music by George C. Stebbins, 1890.

ABOUT THE AUTHOR

Dr. Chris Thurman is a psychologist, an author, and a popular seminar speaker. Chris and his wife, Holly, have been married for thirty-four years and have three children, Matt, Ashley, and Kelly, whom Chris and Holly think hung the moon. In his spare time, Chris is an avid golfer, a Texas Longhorn fan, and a home improvement aficionado.

If you are interested in Chris doing a seminar for your church or organization, please feel free to contact him through his website at drchristhurman.com.

Made in the USA
Monee, IL
08 May 2021